The Opioid Crisis

John Allen

ReferencePoint Press®

San Diego, CA

About the Author

John Allen is a writer who lives in Oklahoma City.

© 2020 ReferencePoint Press, Inc.
Printed in the United States

For more information, contact:
ReferencePoint Press, Inc.
PO Box 27779
San Diego, CA 92198
www.ReferencePointPress.com

LIBRARY OF CONGRESS CATALOGING-IN-PUBLICATION DATA

Name: Allen, John, 1957– author.
Title: The Opioid Crisis/by John Allen.
Description: San Diego, CA: ReferencePoint Press, Inc., 2020. | Series:
    Emerging Issues in Public Health series | Audience: Grade 9 to 12. |
    Includes bibliographical references and index.
Identifiers: LCCN 2018052669 (print) | LCCN 2019007861 (ebook) | ISBN
    9781682826744 (eBook) | ISBN 9781682826737 (hardback)
Subjects: LCSH: Opioid abuse—Juvenile literature. | Opioid
    abuse—Treatment—Juvenile literature. | Drug abuse—Juvenile literature.
    | Drug abuse—Treatment—Juvenile literature.
Classification: LCC RC568.O45 (ebook) | LCC RC568.O45 A45 2020 (print) | DDC
    616.86—dc23
LC record available at https://lccn.loc.gov/2018052669

CONTENTS

A Heavy Toll on Families and Communities

In Houston, Texas, on March 2, 2018, several players for the Rice University football team wondered about a teammate's absence from an informal workout. Blain Padgett, a twenty-one-year-old lineman with great potential, rarely missed a chance to work out with his buddies. A short time later Padgett was found dead in his apartment. An autopsy discovered he had overdosed on a pain-killing drug called carfentanil. This synthetic opioid often looks like powdered cocaine and has ten thousand times the potency of morphine. In a statement about the autopsy's findings, Blain's father expressed grief and confusion. "We would like to know how Blain got his hands on this drug that seems very difficult to get," said Mical Padgett. "That's our main question. How did he get it and why did he take it?"[1]

Communities Searching for Answers

Like Blain Padgett's father, many communities all over the United States find themselves roiled by the growing opioid crisis and searching for answers. The Centers for Disease Control and Prevention (CDC) reports that about seventy-two thousand Americans died from drug overdose in 2017, more than the annual death totals from HIV, car wrecks, or gun violence. That number pertains to all drugs but represents a large percentage of overdose deaths from opioids. In West Virginia, for example, where economic woes have left many workers idle and depressed, opioid abuse is rampant, with the highest overdose death rate in the nation. According to the state's Board of Pharmacy, there were 884 drug overdose deaths in West Virginia in 2016. Reports of this statistic led to calls for change. The following year the number of physician-dispensed doses of painkillers like oxycodone and hydrocodone fell by half. Yet there was still the equivalent of sixty-five doses prescribed for every one of the state's 1.8 million people. And that did not include street sales of other opioids, such as heroin, fentanyl, and carfentanil, which continue to pour into West Virginia cities and towns.

Similar conditions are found in Kentucky, Ohio, New Hampshire, and other states. Jacqueline Zanfagna, a young woman in Plaistow, New Hampshire, became hooked on Vicodin that her mother kept in the medicine cabinet to treat knee pain. Before her parents realized the truth, Jacqueline had begun stealing her mother's jewelry and pawning it for cash she could use to buy cheap heroin from a dealer. Jacqueline eventually died from an overdose of heroin laced with fentanyl. "We know that the people using street drugs—illicit opioids—four out of five started with prescription pills," says Dr. William Goodman, medical director at the Catholic Medical Center in Manchester, New Hampshire. "Often what leads them to go from pills to injection of fentanyl or heroin is that it's easier to get. You don't need a prescription and it's often much less expensive."[2]

> "We know that the people using street drugs—illicit opioids—four out of five started with prescription pills."[2]
>
> —Dr. William Goodman, medical director at the Catholic Medical Center in Manchester, New Hampshire

Like so many families across the nation, Jacqueline's parents agonize over signs they missed and steps they might have taken. Anne Marie Zanfagna, Jacqueline's mother and a gifted artist, has turned to painting portraits of victims like her daughter who fell to opioids. "The first portrait I painted was Jackie," says Zanfagna. "I spent two months painting it. It was like spending time with her. There was joy and there was sorrow."[3]

Drugs That Can Provide Relief or Misery

Opioids are drugs that are prescribed for their ability to relieve pain. Usually given in pill form, they benefit millions of patients by

Blain Padgett, pictured on the sideline at a 2016 Rice University football game, died in 2018 from an overdose of the opioid painkiller carfentanil. His death, like so many others, is part of the tragedy of America's opioid crisis.

easing pain after an operation or reducing acute or chronic pain from an injury or physical condition. Many people use opioid pain killers, like oxycodone and hydrocodone, exactly as directed by their doctors. They stop using them when the pain subsides and never develop an addiction.

Even so, opioids are highly addictive. They provide a flood of endorphins and dopamine, which are neurotransmitters in the brain that trigger feelings of satisfaction and pleasure. This rush of euphoria and happiness is much more concentrated than ordinary feelings of pleasure, leading some users to abuse the drug to get the same high. However, repeated usage dulls the effect. The user must take larger and more frequent doses to experience the same euphoric high. With continued use, a person becomes physically and psychologically dependent on the drug. Stopping the drug results in agonies of withdrawal, including anxiety, cold sweats, sleeplessness, and paranoia. In this state a user will do almost anything to get another dose.

Most opioid addictions begin with a prescription for pain pills. As the drug takes hold, a user may lie about his or her condition to get more pills. When prescriptions run out, the user often turns to street dealers. If pills on the street are too expensive, the user might try heroin, a derivative of morphine that is cooked into liquid and injected with a needle. Deadliest of all the opioids sold on the street today are fentanyl and carfentanil. These synthetic drugs, created in makeshift laboratories, are many times stronger than prescription painkillers and often lead to overdose.

A Complicated Crisis

The growing problem with fentanyl and other synthetic opioids adds one more complication to the opioid crisis in America. Health officials stress that addiction to opioids has no simple solution. Nonetheless, there are stories of progress on many fronts. Some drugmakers are ending their practice of pressuring doctors to prescribe opioids. Doctors themselves are reexamining their habits of prescribing pain medication. Spouses and family members are being urged to look for early signs of opioid abuse. Experts on addiction are devising methods of treating opioid addicts with substance substitution programs that show great promise. Law enforcement officials are trying a fresh approach to neighborhood policing to catch drug dealers. Experts believe it will take a combination of all these efforts to reverse the alarming trend of opioid abuse and save lives. "This is an epidemic of so many epidemics," says West Virginia health commissioner Rahul Gupta. "Just addressing a particular substance of use or misuse isn't enough."[4]

> "This is an epidemic of so many epidemics. Just addressing a particular substance of use or misuse isn't enough."[4]
>
> —West Virginia health commissioner Rahul Gupta

CHAPTER ONE

The Roots of the Opioid Crisis

Purdue Pharma has made billions selling OxyContin, an opioid painkiller, since the company got US Food and Drug Administration (FDA) approval for the drug in 1996. It has also made enemies among addicted patients and their families, politicians, and medical professionals. In June 2018 Massachusetts filed a civil lawsuit against Purdue. The state accused Purdue of misleading patients and doctors about the terrible risks attached to using its pain medications. At a news conference, joined by the governor and law enforcement officials, Massachusetts attorney general Maura Healey spoke with an undercurrent of anger as she announced the suit against Purdue:

> Their strategy was simple: The more drugs they sold, the more money they made—and the more people died. . . . We found that Purdue engaged in a multibillion-dollar enterprise to mislead us about their drugs. Purdue pushed prescribers to give higher doses to keep patients on drugs for longer periods of time, without regard to the very real risks of addiction, overdose and death.[5]

Growing Number of Lawsuits

With its lawsuit, Massachusetts joined a growing number of states intent on punishing drugmakers who they say profit from promoting opioid sales with falsehoods. Similar suits have been filed by twenty-three other states and the territory of Puerto Rico. Massachusetts's effort is different in that it also names top Purdue executives in its filing. About half the people named are members of the Sackler family, which owns the company. Healey believes these individuals are responsible for the company's deceptive marketing—and in turn for helping fuel the national crisis over opioids.

The Massachusetts suit claims Purdue continued to market OxyContin aggressively despite clear evidence that the drug was unsafe. Doctors and patients both recognized that oxycodone, the semisynthetic opioid in OxyContin, is addictive and causes terrible withdrawal pains upon stopping the drug or even between doses.

Purdue Pharma admits that opioid abuse has become a nationwide problem, but the company denies responsibility. It also repeatedly notes that its products are approved by the FDA. In response to a similar suit in Tennessee, Purdue's attorney, William J. Harbison, blamed doctors, patients, and street dealers. "The alleged nuisance in this case is not caused by Purdue's sale of its legal, FDA-regulated medications," Harbison declared, "but rather by doctors who wrote improper prescriptions and/or by third parties who caused persons without valid and medically necessary prescriptions to get opioid medications or illegal street drugs. Purdue has no control over those persons."[6] Despite these claims, Purdue has already made changes in its sales methods. In February 2018 the company cut its sales force in half and ended all direct marketing to doctors.

> "Their strategy was simple: The more drugs they sold, the more money they made—and the more people died. . . . We found that Purdue engaged in a multibillion-dollar enterprise to mislead us about their drugs."[5]
>
> —Maura Healey, attorney general of Massachusetts

A Revolutionary Pain Drug

Purdue Pharma launched OxyContin, its revolutionary drug for pain treatment, with great fanfare in 1996. It met with instant commercial success. From the beginning Purdue Pharma marketed OxyContin aggressively to doctors and pharmacies as a breakthrough in pain relief. Sales ballooned from $48 million to $1.1 billion in its first four years.

To achieve this success Purdue had to change doctors' attitudes about opioids, or pain medications derived from opium. Prior to OxyContin, doctors were reluctant to prescribe opioids because of the well-founded danger of addiction. Only with acute cancer pain or end-of-life pain management were opioids deemed appropriate. However, Purdue set about promoting OxyContin as a safe and effective narcotic for treating moderate to severe pain for a wide range of patients. This was despite the fact that the drug's one active ingredient, oxycodone, is related to heroin and can be twice as powerful as morphine.

According to an investigation by reporters for the *Los Angeles Times*, the company's marketing campaign relied on half-truths and exaggerated claims. Press releases on OxyContin touted its "smooth and sustained pain control all day" and the way it "simplifies and improves patients' lives . . . with twice-daily dosing."[7]

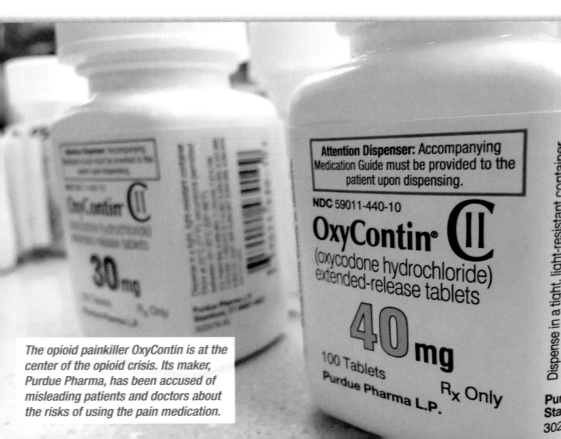

The opioid painkiller OxyContin is at the center of the opioid crisis. Its maker, Purdue Pharma, has been accused of misleading patients and doctors about the risks of using the pain medication.

Specifically, Purdue claimed the drug's painkilling effect would last for twelve to twenty-four hours—a significant advantage over other pain medications, which must be taken more frequently. The extended-release feature was also intended to prevent addiction by allowing the opioid dose to take effect gradually over a period of hours instead of all at once.

The *Los Angeles Times* discovered that for many patients the effect wore off in less than twelve hours—sometimes much less—leaving them with renewed pain and a powerful craving for the drug. Purdue's own clinical trials revealed the truth about OxyContin even before it hit the market, but the company's ads and salespeople continued to push a different story. The company funneled money to advocacy groups to vouch for the drug's long-term effectiveness. Purdue reps urged doctors to prescribe stronger doses, not more frequent ones, to maintain the twelve-hour fiction. This only led to more addicted patients and increased chances of overdose.

A coalition of forty-one states has filed a class-action suit charging that other opioid producers, such as Endo Pharmaceuticals with its oxycodone-based painkiller Percocet, also contributed to the opioid crisis. Yet experts place much of the blame on Purdue Pharma and its aggressive marketing. That campaign led to a profound increase in prescriptions for opioids. "If you look at the prescribing trends for all the different opioids, it's in 1996 that prescribing really takes off," says Andrew Kolodny, codirector of the Opioid Policy Research Collaborative at Brandeis University. "It's not a coincidence. That was the year Purdue launched a multifaceted campaign that misinformed the medical community about the risks."[8]

> "It's in 1996 that prescribing [of OxyContin] really takes off. It's not a coincidence. That was the year Purdue launched a multifaceted campaign that misinformed the medical community about the risks."[8]
>
> —Andrew Kolodny, codirector of the Opioid Policy Research Collaborative at Brandeis University

Soaring Rates of Addiction and Overdose

Promoted as a miracle drug, OxyContin proved to be a scourge for public health. The first patients to receive prescriptions, many of whom had suffered from chronic pain for years, were thrilled at the prospect of a long-acting painkiller that was safe for frequent use. All too often they quickly became disillusioned.

Elizabeth Kipp, a forty-two-year-old mother of two in Kansas City, tried the new drug the first year it was available. Kipp's doctor prescribed it for her back pain, the result of being thrown from a horse as a teenager. She followed directions to the letter, taking a pill every twelve hours. Relief would last only an hour or two. Then her pain would return along with waves of nausea and anxiety. She tried to stick to the twelve-hour regimen, but sometimes in desperation would swallow another pill before the time had elapsed. When Kipp complained, her doctor prescribed stronger doses. Soon she was stuck in a cycle of deep misery and temporary relief—what experts label the perfect formula for addiction. Thoughts of suicide invaded her mind before she finally entered a rehab program. "You want a description of hell," she recalls, "I can give it to you."[9]

> "You want a description of hell, I can give it to you."[9]
>
> —Elizabeth Kipp, who became addicted to OxyContin

Stories like Kipp's played out across the nation. As OxyContin sales increased, rates of addiction and overdose skyrocketed. Soon the pills became popular as street drugs. Users would buy OxyContin illegally from neighborhood dealers and then crush the pills and snort the drug for a rapid high. A Justice Department report obtained by the *New York Times* found that Purdue officials knew what was happening but did nothing. Internal memos show that Purdue salespeople frequently referred to the drug's street value and how it was being crushed and snorted.

Safe or Deadly?

OxyContin is based on an opioid that dates back more than a century. Oxycodone, the active ingredient in OxyContin, is a synthetic opioid first formulated in Germany in 1916. German scientists made oxycodone by modifying morphine, itself a painkiller related to opium. Oxycodone is considered twice as potent as the opiate heroin and no less addictive. It arrived in the United States in 1939 and, under the brand names Percocet, Percodan, and Roxicodone, among others, was prescribed as a fast-acting painkiller to treat moderate to severe pain.

In 1989 the patent for Purdue Pharma's time-released painkiller MS Contin ran out. The company was looking for a follow-up drug to its best seller. In 1995 Purdue won FDA approval for OxyContin, a new time-released pain drug that was based on oxycodone and relatively cheap to produce. In an unusual move, the FDA added a package insert declaring that OxyContin was safer than other painkillers. As reported by the *New Yorker*'s Patrick Radden Keefe, Purdue then embarked on one of the largest ad campaigns in history. Purdue salespeople were taught to obscure the truth about OxyContin, telling skeptical doctors that fewer than 1 percent of patients became addicted. As a result, a highly addictive opioid with deadly potency found its way to medicine cabinets across the nation. For the sake of public health, notes former FDA chief David Kessler, "The goal should have been to sell the least dose of the drug to the smallest number of patients." Instead, Purdue did just the opposite.

Quoted in Patrick Radden Keefe, "The Family That Built an Empire of Pain," *New Yorker*, October 30, 2017. www.newyorker.com.

Misleading the Public

Another victim of OxyContin inspired an organized pushback against Purdue Pharma. In February 2001, eighteen-year-old Eddie Bisch died from an overdose of the drug. His sister found him in their home in Philadelphia, Pennsylvania, nearly blue and unable to respond to her frantic questions. She called their father, Ed Bisch, who raced home to find paramedics parked outside. When Bisch learned his son had died from "Oxy," it was the first time he had heard the name.

Bisch researched the drug and found numerous reports about its deadly effects. His son's overdose had been one of thirty in the area in only the past three months. Bisch contacted other parents who had lost children to OxyContin and shared his feelings of helplessness and outrage. Together they formed Relatives Against Purdue Pharma, or RAPP. Bisch set up an online message board called OxyKills.com to relay news and information about the drug. He reached out to families in the Appalachian region, including the states of West Virginia, Kentucky, and Ohio, where the epidemic seemed most acute. Others joined from as far away as California. RAPP developed into a staunch activist group. Its members lobbied for state programs to monitor opioid prescriptions and marched outside Purdue-sponsored

A sculpture inspired by a family member's battle with opioid addiction is displayed outside Purdue's Connecticut headquarters. Relatives of people who have struggled with or died from opioid addiction are speaking out about the drugmaker's actions.

pain management seminars holding up photos of young overdose victims.

By bringing attention to the OxyContin crisis, RAPP helped spark lawsuits against Purdue Pharma across the nation. At first Purdue brushed aside these civil suits, but estimates of the company's legal bills rose to $3 million a month. One case involved a Purdue sales representative named Karen White, whom the company had fired for supposedly poor communication skills and falling sales. White sued the company for wrongful termination, claiming she was actually fired because she refused to sell to doctors who were overprescribing OxyContin illegally. Although her lawsuit failed, its accusations put Purdue on notice that its business practices faced new scrutiny. "We had such high hopes that [White] would be one of our saviors,"[10] says Barbara Van Rooyan, a RAPP member in California. "They were counting on us to run out of steam," recalls Bisch. "They were lawyered up and Rudy Giuliani'd up."[11]—referring to the well-known former mayor of New York City who was leading Purdue's legal team. However, RAPP's efforts soon began to bear fruit.

A Partial Reckoning

Federal law enforcement officials got involved in the controversy around 2002. In the course of a five-year investigation centered in Virginia, they gathered documents about Purdue sales representative calls in which, they said, fraudulent claims were made about OxyContin. Federal prosecutors believed they had enough evidence to send Purdue executives to prison. "But it got watered down, as it went through the Department of Justice headquarters," says an insider connected to the case, "and the folks working for Purdue, including Giuliani, lobbied hard for the executives not to be indicted on felony charges."[12]

Purdue Pharma could not escape judgment entirely. In 2007 the company paid $634 million in fines after pleading guilty to federal charges of misleading the public about the risks of

OxyContin. Yet afterward, instead of changing its marketing procedures, Purdue doubled down on its pursuit of profits. Purdue salespeople made hundreds of thousands of contacts with doctors and pharmacists nationwide. In 2010 the company adjusted the formula for OxyContin, claiming the new version was safer and much less addictive. Despite this change, the opioid crisis worsened.

Overprescribing Opioids

As opioid painkillers infested American neighborhoods, doctors continued to overprescribe the drugs. Their medical training already prompted doctors to focus on pain relief for patients. Drug companies like Purdue offered strong opioids with the assurance that addiction was unlikely. When OxyContin failed to provide twelve-hour relief as advertised, doctors would increase patients' dosages according to Purdue's recommendations. The desire to relieve patients' agony often backfired, exposing them to even more misery, including the vise grip of addiction, withdrawal symptoms, and the constant danger of overdose.

Meanwhile, the sheer number of opioid prescriptions in the United States exploded. It reached a peak in 2012 with more than 255 million prescriptions, a rate of 81.3 per 100 persons. This was five years after Purdue Pharma had pleaded guilty and paid a huge fine for false advertising of OxyContin. Lawsuits in several states including Tennessee allege that drug companies, seeking to maintain the pace of sales, sent armies of salespeople to pursue doctors, nurse practitioners, and physician assistants. Only doctors could prescribe the drug, but companies sought to influence their staff personnel to apply further pressure. Doctors were plied with free meals and vacation trips, large speaking fees at conferences, and cash for consulting. A 2018 study published in *JAMA Internal Medicine* showed that doctors who received even one meal paid for by an opioid maker were more likely to prescribe opioid painkillers afterward.

Selling Pills for Cash

Some doctors found ways to profit more directly from prescribing opioids. They began to run so-called pill mills out of their offices, selling pain medication like OxyContin directly to street dealers for cash. According to federal law enforcement, by 2011 the street price for a single tablet of OxyContin had risen to fifty to eighty dollars, compared to six dollars per tablet when sold legally. Doctors and pharmacists also were able to double dip on proceeds, since Medicare, Medicaid, and insurance companies reimbursed

Seniors Selling Painkillers

Street dealers of black market opioids have a surprising source for painkilling pills: senior citizens. Law enforcement officials across the country say Americans of retirement age are selling opioids like OxyContin to drug dealers for ready cash. With the recent crackdown on opioids, seniors are one of the few groups that can obtain prescriptions for painkillers with ease because they are thought to be at lower risk for addiction. Patients with a prescription for three pills a day can make as much as $3,600 each month by selling them to a dealer.

This problem has received little notice, partly because prosecutors are reluctant to charge older citizens. Police investigators say juries tend to be shocked to see an older adult on trial and generally hand down light sentences. For example, in January 2017 police discovered more than one hundred oxycodone pills and a significant amount of cash in the home of a seventy-four-year-old woman in Kingsport, Tennessee. The woman received probation for illegally selling prescription pain pills.

Reasons for selling the pills vary. Some seniors may struggle to make ends meet or may face a sudden crisis in their finances. Kent Chitwood, the Kingsport assistant district attorney who prosecuted the case, claims that one-tenth of the prescription drug cases he prosecutes involve older adults. "Some may have economic reasons why they chose to sell their drugs," says Chitwood. "Others have long histories and continue to do these things until their elderly years."

Quoted in Joe Eaton, "The New Opioid Dealers," *AARP Bulletin*, June 2017. www.aarp.org.

A handcuffed suspect is loaded into a police van after a raid on a suspected pill mill in Georgia. Doctors and pharmacists in various states have been arrested and charged with illegally dispensing opioids for profit.

them for all the pills they prescribed and sold, including those sold illegally to black market dealers.

Pill mill arrangements varied from place to place. According to the *Los Angeles Times*, Dr. Alvin Lee, a doctor in Orange County, California, would casually meet supposed patients at a local Starbucks coffeehouse and sell them prescriptions of OxyContin, Vicodin, and Xanax (an opioid commonly prescribed for anxiety) for hundreds of dollars at a time. In 2013 Lee was sentenced to eleven years in prison. Other schemes called for elaborate teamwork. CBS4 in Miami reported that pain clinics in South Florida would fill OxyContin prescriptions for fake patients who obtained the pills for street dealers. While the dealers proceeded to fleece addicted users in back alleys, doctors who made out the original prescriptions received payment from Medicare and private insurers. The Florida scheme became so successful that addicts from other regions were recruited to visit the pain clinics for prescriptions. Many were provided free plane tickets, gift cards, and casino visits for their services. In July 2017 federal officials brought charges against more than four hundred participants nationwide, including dozens of doctors. Florida's legislature responded to the problem with a series of laws designed to break up pill mills in the state.

Doctors in other states have been accused of engaging in similar schemes. A 2018 lawsuit filed by the state of Tennessee alleges that Purdue Pharma targeted pill mill doctors as part of its sales strategy. The lawsuit names four doctors in the Nashville area who allegedly received payments in cash for abnormally large prescriptions of OxyContin. All four had been stripped of their medical licenses in the previous ten years yet somehow regained them and were able to resume their prescribing habits. Authorities claim that despite warnings from pharmacists and police, Purdue salespeople made dozens of calls and visits to these doctors. The flow of OxyContin continued almost until the accused were in handcuffs.

Investigators described in detail the actions of the individuals named in the lawsuit. One couple, Dr. Visuvalingam Vilvarajah and his then wife Dr. Mireille Lalanne, wrote more than sixty-five hundred prescriptions for OxyContin in three years. The prescriptions totaled more than three hundred thousand pills. Another of the accused, Dr. James Pogue, prescribed more OxyContin from 2006 to 2016 than any other doctor in Tennessee. Patients would wait up to nine hours in Pogue's office parking lot to get OxyContin prescriptions. Pogue also prescribed dangerously high dosages of the drug, making it likely the pills were destined for street sales. According to the Tennessee lawsuit, "Dr. Pogue's prolific prescribing habits and use of OxyContin prescription savings cards for cash paying patients were indicative of red flags of which Purdue had knowledge."[13]

> "Dr. Pogue's prolific prescribing habits and use of OxyContin prescription savings cards for cash paying patients were indicative of red flags of which Purdue had knowledge."[13]
>
> — Tennessee lawsuit against Purdue Pharma

A Catastrophe for Public Health

Since Purdue Pharma introduced OxyContin in 1996, perceptions of the opioid painkiller have gone from wonder drug to societal scourge. False claims about the drug's twelve-hour effectiveness led desperate patients to take more pills for relief. Doctors made the situation worse by overprescribing and adding stronger dosages. Soon OxyContin and other opioid painkillers reached the streets, where illegal sales skyrocketed. Lawsuits like the ones in Massachusetts and Tennessee are seeking to punish those responsible for the opioid crisis. For now, an epidemic of addiction and overdose has left families across the United States aching from grief and searching for answers.

CHAPTER TWO

From Pain Pills to Heroin and Fentanyl

On his last, fifty-three-date concert tour, rock star Tom Petty relied on painkillers and a backstage golf cart to nurse his fractured left hip through a grinding routine. Members of his entourage urged him to cancel the tour and check into a hospital. Instead, Petty turned to a mixture of pain medications, including a synthetic opioid called fentanyl. On October 2, 2017, one week after his last show, Petty died from an accidental overdose of painkillers. His system was found to contain three kinds of fentanyl. One was a slow-release patch, but the other two were much more potent variations of the drug. "Those are illicit," says Dr. Nora Volkow of the National Institute on Drug Abuse. "Those you get very likely in the black market."[14]

New Dangers from Fentanyl and Heroin

News of a celebrity's death from overdose helps bring attention to the dangers of new opioids like fentanyl. Petty's family hoped to enlighten the public about the drug, whose potency is thirty to fifty times that of heroin. "It is so crazy-strong," says Petty's daughter Adria. "We really don't want this to happen to anyone else. We learned this is the worst feeling you can have: to lose someone you love for no good reason."[15]

Petty was not the first music legend to succumb to fentanyl. On April 21, 2016, Prince was found alone and unresponsive in an elevator at his Paisley Park studio in Minnesota. Addicted to opioid painkillers since a 2010 hip surgery, the performer apparently had taken fentanyl in pill form in the mistaken belief that it was Vicodin, a less potent drug. "In all likelihood, Prince had no idea he was taking a counterfeit pill that could kill him," said Carver County district attorney Mark Metz following an investigation. "Prince's death is a tragic example that opioid addiction, and overdose deaths do not discriminate no matter the demographic."[16]

President Donald Trump has called for tougher penalties related to fentanyl. He has even suggested the death penalty for dealers found to have sold the drug to the victim of a fatal overdose. Nonetheless, others doubt that tougher law enforcement is the answer. Prince's sister, Tyka Nelson, did not object when the state of Minnesota declined to arrest anyone for the fentanyl that killed her brother. "I thought, 'Let's move on,'" she says. "You can charge 20,000 people and toss them in jail. Will that bring my brother back?"[17]

As fentanyl has gained notoriety as a lethal painkiller, a better-known narcotic has also been contributing to the opioid crisis. Heroin, once considered a drug limited to hard-core junkies in the inner city, today is sold to middle-class suburban addicts who originally fell victim to oxycodone. Some dealers peddle heroin laced with fentanyl to form an even more potent cocktail. Often users have no idea the heroin they are buying is in part or mostly fentanyl. Those who think they have a tolerance for heroin end up overdosing on the vastly more potent combination. According to the National Institute on Drug Abuse, deaths from opioid overdose have jumped as a result. In 2017 there were 29,406 fatal overdoses of synthetic opioids like fentanyl and 15,958 from heroin. Americans are starting to realize that what began as a prescription drug crisis has expanded to include a variety of deadly opioids.

> "Prince's death is a tragic example that opioid addiction, and overdose deaths do not discriminate no matter the demographic."[16]
>
> —Carver County, Minnesota, district attorney Mark Metz

Unintended Consequences

The surge in heroin and fentanyl abuse is partly the result of a change to OxyContin. In 2010 Purdue Pharma introduced a reformulated version of the drug. This change was intended to

US Deaths from Opioid Overdose Continue to Rise

Overdose deaths caused by opioids reached an all-time high in the United States in 2017. The sharpest increase in opioid-related deaths in 2017 resulted from the synthetic opioid fentanyl. Overdose deaths from heroin and prescription painkillers have also increased, although not as steeply.

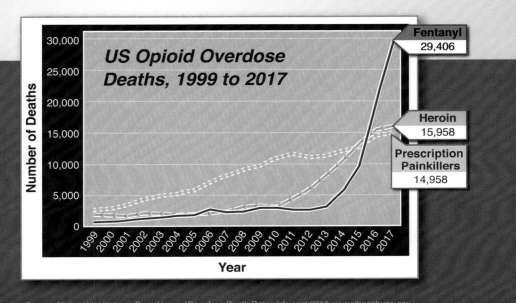

US Opioid Overdose Deaths, 1999 to 2017

Number of Deaths

Fentanyl
29,406

Heroin
15,958

Prescription Painkillers
14,958

Year

Source: National Institute on Drug Abuse, "Overdose Death Rates," August 2018. www.drugabuse.gov.

make the painkiller safer and less likely to be abused by addicts. Instead, according to law enforcement experts, it sent addicted OxyContin users in search of more powerful opioids.

With the original version of OxyContin, addicts could crush the pills into powder and either snort the powder or, in liquefied form, inject it. They would then receive the full dosage almost at once, with no time-release delay. Many street buyers of OxyContin used it in this way to get a rapid and powerful high. This helped make OxyContin a huge success on the black market. To curtail this abuse and discourage street sales, Purdue changed the drug's formula. Crushing the new pills turns them into a gummy substance that is more difficult for users to snort or inject. Other makers of time-release opioids have introduced similar changes.

Although Purdue's reformulation of OxyContin was aimed at curbing addiction, the effort seems to have backfired. The reformulated drug costs more than older versions, which might lead some individuals to seek cheaper—and more dangerous—alternatives on the street. Additionally, opioid addicts grown accustomed to almost immediate highs turned to other, more potent substances that could satisfy their needs. Rates of overdose from heroin began to climb, even quadrupling in several areas. A 2018 study published by the National Bureau of Economic Research suggests that Purdue's efforts were mostly wasted. "As people decided OxyContin was too much of a hassle, some former OxyContin users moved on to heroin," says science reporter German Lopez. "The subsequent rise in heroin overdose deaths may have been enough, the researchers argued, to match or even outweigh any good that the reformulation of OxyContin did in terms of preventing painkiller overdose deaths—at least in the short term."[18] Overall the attempt to head off one epidemic has led to the growth of another, centered on heroin and fentanyl.

Heroin's Comeback

News reports stress that heroin is making a comeback on American streets as part of the opioid crisis. In reality, heroin never left. It has a long history in the United States, dating back more than a century. "The current opioid crisis may have been jump-started with prescription drugs, but heroin came long before OxyContin," says Roger Chriss, a Washington State University technical consultant who has studied patterns of prescribing painkillers in America. "It is better to view OxyContin as gasoline tossed on a smoldering fire."[19]

The National Institute on Drug Abuse estimates there are one-half million heroin addicts today in the United States. Experts say this is roughly the same level as in the 1990s and 1970s. What has made the problem worse today is the wide availability of other

The Xalisco Boys

One of the largest distributors of heroin in the United States is a gang located in the small town of Xalisco on the Pacific coast of Mexico. The Xalisco Boys, as author Sam Quinones calls them, have streamlined sales of heroin into a reliable business that is almost like pizza delivery, only massively more profitable. The gang focuses on black tar heroin, a less processed form manufactured from Mexican-grown poppies. Compared to Asian varieties, black tar heroin is much cheaper to produce and transport. As a result, it can be sold for a lower price. Users of OxyContin are therefore enticed to switch to heroin and become regular customers.

The Xalisco Boys avoid violence with other gangs, and their drivers do not carry guns. They focus on midsize cities, prosperous but low-key, where business can proceed in an orderly manner. The routine is remarkably similar in every city or town. Dealers are given a phone number to pass around. When an addict calls, an operator sends him or her to a parking lot or street corner. The operator notifies a driver, who hustles to make the connection. The driver has a mouthful of heroin in tiny balloons, with a bottle of water at hand to wash down the balloons should the police stop him. He finds the customer, spits out the proper number of balloons, and receives the money. According to Quinones, such transactions occur each day from 7:00 a.m. to 7:00 p.m.—because the Xalisco Boys keep regular business hours.

opioids that can act as a gateway to heroin use. Sales of heroin may have dropped off temporarily when prescription painkillers became plentiful on the street. But they have roared back in response to efforts to control distribution of OxyContin and other opioid pain pills. Addicts desperate to ward off the agony of withdrawal have turned to heroin for less expensive fixes. According to Beth Macy, author of *Dopesick*, a book about the opioid crisis, "Four out of five heroin addicts come to the drugs . . . through prescribed opioids."[20]

Users also are introduced to heroin by pill dealers who tout heroin as a cheap substitute offering more potency. Erin Marie Daly, a journalist who has interviewed dozens of young opioid users, says friends often relay the advice: "The minute one friend said, 'Hey, my dealer hooked me up with this awesome, super cheap stuff—try it,' the kids would try it. Once they tried heroin, there was no going back. Even if they wanted to stop, they were physically unable."[21]

Typical is the case of Andi Peterson, a middle-class young woman in Weber County, Utah. Peterson first took opioid painkillers at age sixteen. A couple of years later, she and a boyfriend would share a bottle of Percocet over the course of a week. "I remember feeling really good and comfortable in my own skin for once," says Peterson. "I felt like I could talk to people."[22] Soon, at her boyfriend's suggestion, they moved on to smoking heroin. After six months her highway patrolman stepdad noticed her fidgeting and sweating. Confessing her heroin use, Peterson agreed to enter a rehab program. At first her cravings overcame her good intentions. She returned to her boyfriend and her heroin habit, this time via injection. It took Peterson several tries before she was finally able to take advantage of treatment and escape the drug's powerful grip.

Deadly Risks for a Rush

Among the world's most addictive narcotics, heroin is derived from opium, which is made from the seeds of the poppy plant. Heroin is produced in three major regions of the world: eastern Asia, western Asia, and Latin America. Afghanistan, a country of 34 million people in western Asia, is the world's largest supplier. Most heroin distributed and sold in the United States comes from Latin America. A less pure version frequently found on the streets, called black tar heroin, is manufactured in Mexico.

Like OxyContin, heroin was originally considered a wonder drug, safe enough to be prescribed for colds and headaches. In 1924, after scientists established its highly addictive nature, Congress banned the sale and use of heroin. Since it was outlawed, heroin has been a profitable drug for illegal trafficking in the United States.

In appearance, heroin can be a fine white or brown powder or a sticky black goo. Most users snort or smoke the drug. Opioid addicts seeking the quickest, most potent high inject it directly into a vein, a process called mainlining or shooting up. Once in the bloodstream, the drug delivers its rush of euphoria within seconds. After the initial rush comes a period in which the user thinks and moves more slowly, as if in a dream. Heart rate and breathing also slow down, sometimes dangerously so. An overdose can stop a person's breathing altogether.

Taking heroin in any manner is hazardous, but shooting up heroin carries with it a number of terrible risks. A user may contract

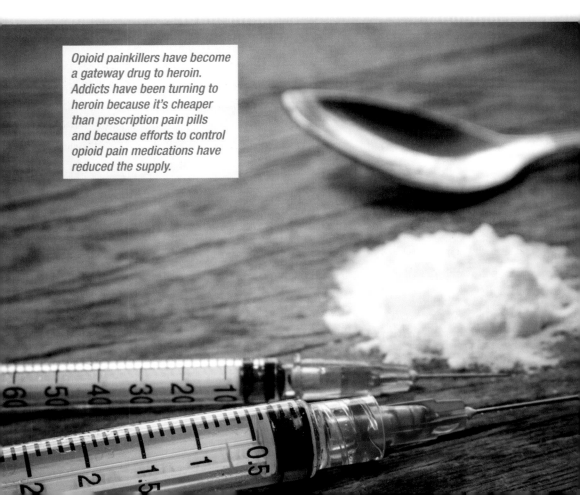

Opioid painkillers have become a gateway drug to heroin. Addicts have been turning to heroin because it's cheaper than prescription pain pills and because efforts to control opioid pain medications have reduced the supply.

HIV, hepatitis, or some other blood-borne disease from a shared needle. Further, introducing such a powerful narcotic straight into the bloodstream is a recipe for overdose. If the heroin is mixed, or cut, with other drugs, injecting it only increases the chance of a fatal mistake.

An Even More Dangerous Opioid

The deadliest addition to heroin today is fentanyl. Dealers seeking to maximize profits from a supply of heroin often mix it with cheaper fentanyl that is manufactured illicitly. That way they can dilute the heroin and still maintain the overall potency. The ever-present danger to users comes from not knowing exactly what they are getting. They may actually be purchasing a dose of fentanyl more powerful than anything they have ever taken. Those who believe they have a tolerance for straight heroin may shortly be lying in an unresponsive heap after overdosing on fentanyl-laced heroin. "Dope is cut so many different ways now that you don't know . . . [what is] in it," says Tony Parilla, a New Yorker

Federal officials display confiscated bags of fentanyl. Illicit drugmakers have been adding fentanyl and fake fentanyl to heroin, creating an especially potent—and often deadly—mix.

who began shooting heroin as a teenager. "And with fentanyl, you can't really tell until you shoot it."[23]

Fentanyl was created in 1959 to manage postsurgical pain or treat patients with severe chronic pain. It consists of a specific formula and is only made in certified labs. The fake fentanyl found on the streets today is mostly made in hidden laboratories in China, Mexico, and Latin America. With no controls, it can be cooked up to almost any strength. Dealers sell this illicit brand of fentanyl in many forms, including a powder, a tablet that resembles milder painkillers, or a blotter paper. Users swallow, snort, or inject the powder or crushed tablets. The blotter-paper dose is placed in the user's mouth and absorbed through the mucous membrane.

Experts say fentanyl's potent punch is responsible for the spike in overdose deaths in many regions of the nation. Fentanyl is many times more powerful than heroin because of its chemical structure. It pierces the fatty blood-brain barrier, which helps keep harmful substances away from the brain, much more quickly than heroin. This enables it to impact the user's central nervous system very rapidly. More important, it takes very little fentanyl to get a lethal dose—micrograms, as opposed to milligrams with other opioids. For example, a lethal amount of heroin looks like half a packet of sugar; a lethal dose of fentanyl, like a few scattered granules. Users overdose from depressed breathing, as with other painkillers, except with fentanyl it happens very fast. Victims suddenly are gripped by what seems like paralysis. "If anything can be likened to a weapon of mass destruction in what it can do to a community, it's fentanyl," says Michael Ferguson, the special agent in charge of the US Drug Enforcement Administration's New England division. "It's manufactured death."[24]

> "Dope is cut so many different ways now that you don't know . . . [what is] in it. And with fentanyl, you can't really tell until you shoot it."[23]
>
> —Tony Parilla, a New Yorker who began shooting heroin as a teenager

A Grim Reputation

There is no shortage of stories about first-time users of fentanyl or fentanyl-laced heroin succumbing to overdose. Even among opioid addicts, fake fentanyl has acquired a grim reputation. As a precaution, some get testing strips from a needle-exchange center that enable them to test a drug for the presence of fentanyl. A few even carry their own kits of Narcan, an effective antidote for opioid overdose, in case they encounter a dangerously strong dose of fentanyl. They know that dealers now also mix fentanyl

An Opioid Not Meant for Humans

As if fentanyl was not problem enough, another even more potent opioid has invaded American streets. Carfentanil is the most powerful commercial opioid in the world. Marketed under the name Wildnil, it is used to sedate elephants and other large animals. With a potency one hundred times that of fentanyl, carfentanil is not intended for human use. Nonetheless, the drug has gone from clandestine labs to mail-order sales and street dealers. A tiny amount—0.02 milligrams, or scarcely more than a couple of grains of sand—could be fatal to an unsuspecting user.

By tweaking the fentanyl molecule, illicit labs in China are producing lethal new opioid compounds like carfentanil. These synthetic drugs, often added to heroin, are showing up around the country. For as little as $750, a person can make an online purchase of 100 grams of Chinese-produced carfentanil, to be delivered overnight by secret courier. According to Richard A. Friedman, a psychopharmacologist in New York City, this is enough for 5 million fatal overdoses.

Like an approaching storm, carfentanil obliges drug agents to brace for its impact. When a 1-kilogram package of carfentanil was intercepted in the Canadian city of Calgary, officials in Cincinnati, Ohio, realized the deadly drug would soon be making its way to their own streets. "We were hearing about something so dastardly we had to be prepared," says Lakshmi Sammarco, the coroner for Hamilton County in Ohio. "We all looked at each other and said, 'Alright, buckle your seat belts, this is going to get very bumpy.'"

Quoted in Kathleen McLaughlin, "Underground Labs in China Are Devising Potent New Opiates Faster than Authorities Can Respond," *Science*, March 29, 2017. www.sciencemag.org.

with cocaine, meth, and other drugs. They have learned the signs of fentanyl overdose: confusion, choking, vomiting, seizures, blue-tinted lips or nails, and shallow breathing.

Yet opioid addicts often are too woozy or addled to discern when a dealer is slipping them fake fentanyl. Small dealers who are users themselves may not be fully aware of what they are selling. Other dealers routinely add fake fentanyl to their latest supply of heroin. For drug gangs and dealers, the economics of peddling fentanyl are hard to resist. A kilogram of heroin brings about $200,000 on the street. Cutting the heroin with a few thousand dollars' worth of fake fentanyl can easily boost those proceeds into the millions. If a certain number of customers overdose from the mixture, there are always new ones ready to make a connection.

As painkiller users have migrated to heroin and fentanyl, the opioid crisis in the United States has gotten worse. Attempts to stop the overprescribing of OxyContin and other pain pills has inadvertently spurred the sales of other, more deadly opioids. According to preliminary figures from the CDC, 2017 was the worst year yet for drug overdose deaths in the United States. As long as more and stronger opioids continue to be distributed on the street, this trend seems likely to continue.

CHAPTER THREE

The Human Toll of Opioid Addiction

On a Saturday afternoon in August 2018, Kevin Bush received a phone call he had half expected and long dreaded. The body of his daughter, Destiny Williams, had just been found dumped behind a closed, ramshackle restaurant in her hometown of Middletown, Ohio. Williams, twenty-four, was dead of an apparent heroin overdose. Troubled by drugs for years, the mother of four young children had been addicted to heroin, kicked the habit, then started on meth before finally getting clean for several months. For her father, whom she always called Pops, Williams's end as one more drug statistic was heartbreaking. "She was thrown away like a bag of trash," says Bush. "She was far from trash. She is someone's mother, sister, and daughter."[25]

A Painfully Familiar Story

Williams's death from opioid abuse is a story that has become painfully familiar in American cities and towns. In the Appalachian belt, where Middletown is typical, news reports of overdose from painkillers, heroin, fentanyl, and other opioids rush past in a seeming blur. Practically everyone knows one of the victims—a friend from high school, a fellow church member, the kid who used to mow the yard, one of the bridesmaids in a family wedding. Taken together, the deaths form a frightening picture of a situation that is out of control.

Statistics provide a grim reminder of the daily toll. According to the CDC, Americans are by far the world's largest consumers of opioids, both natural and synthetic. Each year health care providers in the United States write more than 200 million prescriptions for opioid pain medications. Every day more than one thousand people are treated in American emergency rooms for misuse of opioids. Opioid abuse is the leading cause of death for Americans under age fifty. About 116 people die each day from opioid overdose. And from 1999 to 2016 (the last year for which statistics are available), deaths from opioid overdose in the Appalachian states of Kentucky, Ohio, and West Virginia rose more than 1,000 percent.

Besides the human cost, there is also the growing economic burden. The CDC estimates the total cost to the nation of prescription opioid abuse—including health care, lost productivity, treatment for addiction, and criminal justice—at $78.5 billion annually. According to the Council of Economic Advisers, all the costs associated with the opioid crisis add up to more than $500 billion each year.

At the *Journal-News*, Middletown's local newspaper, reporters comb through the numbers for the city—966 opioid-related overdoses in 2017, 77 of them fatal—and try to make sense of them for their readers. Locals show up for town meetings to discuss the causes of the epidemic, what can be done to combat it, and how each of them has been affected. Among those in attendance are addicts, parents of addicts, emergency room nurses, and social workers. They discuss the need for more detox and treatment centers and the stigma about opioid addiction that keeps users from seeking help. The goal is to prevent young addicts like Williams from becoming just another painful statistic. Danette Moore, who has two sons addicted to opioids, appreciates the opportunity to share ideas with neighbors.

> "You need to understand that you'll walk a fine line of being an enabler and tough love. You'll also learn that you don't have control over the situation, even if you wanted to."[26]
>
> —Danette Moore, who has two sons addicted to opioids

Asked her advice for other parents of addicts, Moore says, "You need to understand that you'll walk a fine line of being an enabler and tough love. You'll also learn that you don't have control over the situation, even if you wanted to."[26]

Joblessness and Addiction

In many areas, opioid abuse is connected to unemployment and despair. Twenty-three-year-old Tyler Moore used to work security at a coal-mining company in Lovely, Kentucky, but lost his job after failing a drug test. Adrift and depressed, he moved into a battered camper set on cinder blocks behind his parents' house. Like his unemployed neighbors and friends, he began to abuse his prescription pain meds. He became addicted, recklessly got into fights, and spent time in jail. Now, with the coal mines closing and other businesses disappearing, Moore cannot find work. About his Oxy-Contin habit, he says, "I guess I used it as my crutch, in a way."[27]

It is no coincidence that the opioid crisis has struck Appalachia and the so-called Rust Belt especially hard. The past decade has seen closings of factories, mines, and steel mills across several Appalachian states, including Kentucky, Ohio, Pennsylvania, and West Virginia. Economic uncertainty turned to hopelessness, as companies that had provided jobs for generations of workers moved manufacturing facilities overseas or closed down

Steel mills, coal mines, and factories (such as this Kraft Foods factory in Allentown, Pennsylvania) have closed in parts of Appalachia, throwing thousands of people out of work. Experts have linked economic despair in this region to an increase in opioid addiction.

due to mismanagement or pressures from foreign competition. Padlocked factories and abandoned mines became symbols of the region's growing misery. For every job lost at a steel mill or coal mine, ten other jobs eventually vanished in the fading small towns. Jobless workers all too often turned to opioids to escape their anger and frustration. And just as factory jobs used to be passed down from one generation to the next, opioid addiction has also found its way from parents to teenagers and young adults.

In 2017 researchers at the University of Chicago's Walsh Center for Rural Health Analysis published a report on the links between economic despair and opioid abuse in Appalachia. They noted that addiction was worst among males in the prime years of their working life. Too often, those who cannot find jobs succumb to boredom and depression. They turn to opioids to mask their feelings of worthlessness. "As we think about challenges that the Appalachian communities face in terms of rebuilding their economies, losing your workforce in the prime of their working years makes that a much more difficult challenge," says Michael Meit, one of the authors of the report. "As we think about how we solve this problem, part of it is treating people already addicted, but the next part is preventing the next group."[28]

> "As we think about how we solve this problem, part of it is treating people already addicted, but the next part is preventing the next group."[28]
>
> —Michael Meit, coauthor of a study on economic despair and opioid abuse

From Pain Management to Deadly Habit

Jeffrey Stevens, an unemployed coal miner in Huntington, West Virginia, was one of those already addicted when he finally hit rock bottom. Roaming the woods naked while high on OxyContin and meth, Stevens spotted a four-wheeler parked beside a farmhouse. He decided to take the vehicle for a joyride, unaware it was the property of the county sheriff. A security camera captured his naked antics, and thirty-nine-year-old Stevens wound up in jail.

Like many other mine workers, Stevens had started using OxyContin to deal with aches and injuries incurred in the depths of the coal mine. Too many other miners were taking pain pills for anyone to notice Stevens's habit. And keeping a valid prescription for OxyContin was easy with so many pill mills in the vicinity. "A coal miner's got good insurance," says Stevens, "so you could find doctors that would throw anything at you."[29]

As Stevens's experience shows, another factor in the opioid crisis is the grinding type of labor performed in Appalachia and other hard-hit areas. Mining, lumbering, manufacturing, and oil and gas fieldwork involve hazards that often leave employees with painful injuries. Coal miners spend hours contorted in precarious holes underground, leaving them with chronic neck and back pain. Some resort to painkillers like OxyContin just to continue on the job. Others, whose injuries are more severe and prevent them from working, may receive workers' compensation, which usually includes prescriptions for heavy-duty opioids with few limits.

Either way, many workers end up in a long-term cycle of opioid abuse and addiction. John Temple, a professor at West Virginia University and author of the book *American Pain*, blames mining company policies for making the problem worse. "In a mining camp, there aren't a lot of doctors," says Temple. "That doctor is going to be more likely to opt for the quick fix and give people pills to fix their pain and get them back into the mine, rather than give them rest or therapy or those things that can actually cure pain."[30] Such policies also can endanger others on the job since workers impaired by painkillers are more likely to cause a serious accident.

A Ripple Effect

Easy access to opioids and the addiction that follows can send shock waves through families. Users find their lives spiraling out

Kentucky coal miners who have completed their shift underground get a ride back to the staging area. Work-related pain and injuries lead many miners and others in labor-intensive jobs to seek relief through opioid painkillers.

of control, and parents and loved ones struggle to cope with the personal wreckage. Thirty-seven-year-old Stephanie Forrester started taking pain pills after her mother's death. When the prescription pills became too expensive, she and her husband switched to heroin bought on the street. They would swipe anything to get money for drugs, even stealing from friends. If necessary, Forrester would resort to prostitution. The couple's two children were raised in the midst of addiction and chaos. As Forrester recalls, "When my husband, Justin, and I were using, at first we'd try to hide it from our kids. But it started coming to the point where the kids would just come into the room. We would tell them to leave, but it didn't really matter anymore. They had witnessed us shooting up."[31]

Eventually, Forrester's opioid habit damaged every relationship in her life. She split with her husband and quarreled with longtime friends. Her father grew distant, returning only to take custody of her children. Finally, she went to jail for theft. There she met Dr. Tisha Smith, director of drug and alcohol rehabilitation for the Monroe County Sheriff's Office in New York. Smith has seen plenty of these situations, in which users feel abandoned with no circle of support. "I've seen families ripped apart because of this," says Smith. "The ripple effect is huge. It is affecting these women's families. It's typically affecting their parents, their siblings, their significant others."[32]

> "I've seen families ripped apart because of [opioid abuse]. The ripple effect is huge."[32]
>
> —Dr. Tisha Smith, director of drug and alcohol rehabilitation in Monroe County, New York

In lockup Forrester was able to get clean and, with Smith's guidance, overcome feelings of guilt and shame. Once sober, she had to face a new reality. She learned about the deaths of several people she had loved, including her husband. Today she is working to reconnect with her father and regain custody of her kids. She is also starting her own nonprofit group to help opioid addicts with free meals, clean needles, and advice for drug treatment.

Mothers on Opioids

Another growing problem is young women who are having babies despite being addicted to opioids. Researchers at Vanderbilt University Medical Center say that every fifteen minutes in the United States a baby is born with symptoms of withdrawal from opioids. Doctors and social workers fear the consequences, both immediate and long term, for babies born to a mother dealing with opioid addiction. The physical and emotional effects are still largely unknown.

Twenty-five-year-old Amanda Williammee has been hooked on opioid painkillers since she was in college, six years ago. She has two daughters, two-year-old Taycee and six-month-old Jayde. During both pregnancies, Williammee repeatedly injected opioids. As a result, both babies were born with neonatal abstinence syndrome. Like an addict with withdrawal symptoms, they had to suffer through tremors, irritability, and sleeplessness. Their bouts of high-pitched crying seemed endless. Although both

Booming Business for Pharmacies

In many regions of the United States, hazardous and physically taxing jobs are still the norm. As the number of injured and disabled workers rises, so does the number of pharmacies to dispense pain medication. With so many opioids available, they pass into the hands of not only miners and steel mill workers but also waitresses, short-order cooks, plumbers, mechanics, and anyone else who might be depressed or simply bored. Manchester, Kentucky, a struggling town in the foothills of the Appalachian Mountains, is a good example. Although a small town of only fifteen hundred people, Manchester has eleven pharmacies, four of which opened in the past three years. For Daniel Gray, a pharmacist at the Family Drug Center located in a run-down Manchester strip mall, business is thriving. "Pain," says Gray, "is big in this area."

These drugstores offer almost no merchandise over the counter like the national chains. Their business is filling prescriptions for the residents of surrounding Clay County. In one twelve-month period, Clay residents were prescribed 2.2 million doses of hydrocodone and 617,000 doses of oxycodone, which is about 150 for every adult and child in the county. According to Jeffrey Newswanger, an emergency room physician and chief medical officer at Manchester Memorial Hospital, "Doctors are under tremendous pressure to prescribe and patients wear you down."

Quoted in Phil Galewitz, "The Pharmacies Thriving in Kentucky's Opioid-Stricken Towns," *Atlantic*, February 7, 2017. www.theatlantic.com.

babies were affected, Taycee's condition was worse. "It wasn't just like we had this two-week period at the hospital of her being sick," says Williammee. "It went on for months because she did not sleep."[33]

Williammee's children go to a day care facility sponsored by the University of North Carolina Medical Center. While her daughters are there, Williammee attends classes and therapy sessions designed to help her kick her drug habit. So far, Taycee and Jayde seem to have escaped some of the problems researchers have found related to children exposed to opioids in the womb. These include a tendency to need treatment for lazy eye by age three

A Missouri woman feeds her ten-month-old grandson, who was born with an opioid addiction. Health officials have witnessed an increase in the number of babies born to opioid-addicted mothers.

and lower scores in cognitive, language, and motor skills. The best outcome for the girls would be for Williammee herself to get clean and steer clear of the drug-addled chaos that can wreck children's lives. A child protection agency has warned Williammee she could lose custody if she fails to break free from opioid addiction. Through it all Williammee is hopeful. "I'm not just some drug addict," she says. "I'm a mother of two kids. And I feel like I'm a great mother. I have educational goals I plan to accomplish, and I plan on being a productive human being in our society."[34]

Mounting Costs to Families

Along with the emotional toll of opioid addiction, families must also cope with financial pressures that can be devastating. The Johnsons of Muncie, Indiana, were overjoyed when their twenty-seven-year-old daughter, Destini, returned home after two months in jail on drug charges. However, Destini's apparent determination to get clean and find work soon fell away, and she began to abuse opioids once more. Eight months after leaving jail, Destini overdosed, suffered a dozen strokes, and wound up in a coma. Day after day her mother, Katiena, waited at the intensive care unit at Muncie's Ball Memorial Hospital. Not only was Katiena fearful for her daughter's survival and fretting about the likelihood of brain damage, she also dreaded the thought of how she and

A Role for Grandparents of Addicts

The opioid crisis has led many grandparents to take custody of their grandchildren while a son or daughter goes through rehab or does jail time for drug offenses. Marvin Sirbu and his wife, Ann Sinsheimer, assumed temporary custody of their granddaughters, Brooklyn and Skylar, while their opioid-addicted daughter enrolled in a rehab program. What started as a commitment of a few months has now extended to three years. It had been quite a while since the older couple had raised children, but they figured they could get the hang of it easily enough. That was before Brooklyn, strongly attached to her missing mother, began to throw screaming tantrums. And then Skylar, living with memories of her drugged parents' violent quarrels, began to twitch wildly at bedtime and cry out in her sleep.

Sirbu is still getting accustomed to the strain of being responsible for young children again. He frets about the alarm going off and about getting the girls to school on time. He worries about his health and the prospects for his addicted daughter. Still, Sirbu and his wife are performing a valuable service. They are able to comfort the girls and help them overcome the trauma of their formerly chaotic lives. "We do know from work and studies that have been done on trauma that grandparents really can and do play a [protective] role," says Donna Butts, executive director of Generations United, an advocacy group for children, youth, and older adults. "And because of that, they offer the children a sense of familiarity and stability."

Quoted in Brit McCandless Farmer, "When Opioids Impact the Whole Family," *60 Minutes Overtime*, August 19, 2018. www.cbsnews.com.

her husband would pay for the mounting costs of Destini's opioid disaster. "Her troubles just kept piling on top of one and the other and the other and the other," says Katiena. "They just bury [themselves] deeper and deeper in cost after cost after cost, of court costs and everything else."[35]

Money worries add to the family's anxiety about their daughter. Even before her last overdose, Katiena and her husband had missed many days of work to drive Destini to treatment centers and rehab. They cared for Destini's two toddlers, paid her court costs and legal fees, and put off retirement to cover the extra expenses. Even with insurance, this latest overdose was going to bring further bills for emergency services, hospitalization, and probably nursing care and physical therapy. Destini did regain consciousness and was removed from intensive care. Her parents are grateful, but their daughter's condition is tenuous. They know she might die long before the bills stop coming.

Destiny Williams and Destini Johnson are examples of the human toll of the opioid crisis. Areas of the country awash in pain pills and heroin have seen frightening increases in addiction and fatal overdose. Across Appalachia workers in hazardous industries take painkillers to get through the workday. Those who lose their jobs either from injury or shutdowns often fall into chronic abuse of opioids. Addicted young women even pass on their withdrawal symptoms to their babies. In the end it is families and loved ones who must bear the burden of this terrible epidemic.

CHAPTER FOUR

Policing the Opioid Crisis

Huntington, West Virginia, is a city besieged with opioid abuse. But Huntington is trying a new approach to the problem. Each morning a team of responders takes to the streets to contact overdose victims. The team consists of three members: police officer Chris Trembley, paramedic Larrecsa Cox, and Sue Howland, who works for Prestera, a mental health service specializing in addiction treatment. Their first stop on a spring day in 2018 is the home of a twenty-six-year-old woman who overdosed on opioids the week before. Staying with her grandparents, she is depressed, anxious, and still a bit suspicious of the team. This is their third visit since the overdose, and they are gradually gaining her trust. They ask about her appetite and whether her headaches have subsided. They hope to convince her to enter a drug treatment program. The visit lasts only ten minutes, but the team members feel they are making progress. Trembley sees it as a small victory for them and the young woman. "Maybe you just didn't go use today," says Trembley. "That's one day. Maybe you might have used but because folks have talked to you and you were feeling good about things maybe you didn't go out and shoplift today. OK, that's still a thing."[36]

Forming a Quick Response Team

Huntington's new procedure with overdose cases is called a quick response team (QRT). The idea is currently being tested in several cities across the country. Bob Hansen, who started the program in Huntington, first read about the team approach in an article about the police department in Colerain, Ohio. Hansen set up a training session with the heads of the Colerain program and loved the approach. He applied for and received two federal grants to pay for the experiment. "We've been having a lot of overdoses in Huntington and Cabell County and really the big thing that stood out to many of us is what are we doing afterwards?"[37] says Hansen. Too often, the next time the police would see an overdose victim is when the person was lying dead on the bathroom floor with a needle stuck in his or her arm.

Teaming an officer with medical and mental health professionals gets across the message to opioid addicts that the purpose is not punishment but care. Fanning out over the city, the team checks on the health of overdose victims and urges them to get professional help. After only four months, the Huntington team has convinced 40 percent of the addicts it has visited to enroll in a treatment program. Other cities are seeing similar results. Charlie Kilbel, a paramedic with a QRT in Cuyahoga Falls, Ohio, is excited

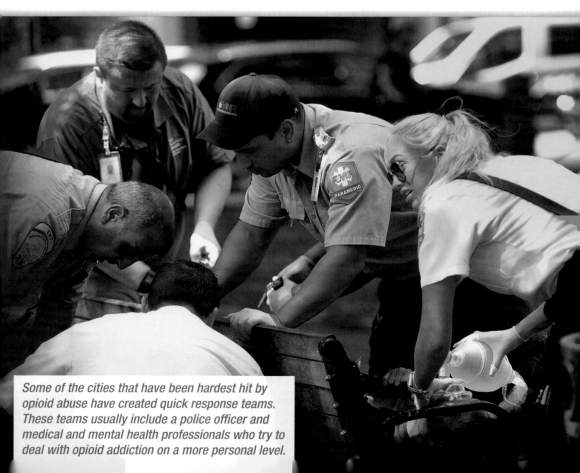

Some of the cities that have been hardest hit by opioid abuse have created quick response teams. These teams usually include a police officer and medical and mental health professionals who try to deal with opioid addiction on a more personal level.

about the chance to bring hope to opioid users. "Our goal is to be at the doorstep of overdose victims within 6 days of their overdose," says Kilbel, "and we will get the individual to detox and/or treatment as long as they're ready. If they don't answer the door or they're not ready we will continue to go back until they do."[38] Success has encouraged other towns to adopt the program, not only in West Virginia and Ohio but across the nation.

> "Our goal is to be at the doorstep of overdose victims within 6 days of their overdose, and we will get the individual to detox and/or treatment as long as they're ready."[38]
>
> —Charlie Kilbel, a paramedic with a QRT in Cuyahoga Falls, Ohio

A Welcome Change

Many experts in health care and law enforcement see programs like Huntington's QRT as a welcome change in dealing with the opioid crisis. They observe that tougher policing has failed to curb drug epidemics in the past and has had little effect on the current opioid problem. A better approach, they say, is to treat opioid addicts as victims who need help rather than criminals who deserve jail time. Rather than focus strictly on law enforcement solutions, they suggest a comprehensive approach that also includes education, prevention, treatment, and recovery. Nan Whaley, the mayor of Dayton, Ohio, where a QRT program is making inroads against a dire opioid problem, agrees a change is needed:

> Locking up people suffering from addiction does nothing. Instead, this reflex toward punishment perpetuates the misuse and overuse of jails that continues to drive over-incarceration at huge cost to taxpayers and untold costs to families and communities. . . . Treating addiction as a public health problem—not a criminal justice one—is key to this success, as communities across the country are already demonstrating. Outdated thinking won't work and families suffering through this crisis deserve better.[39]

Despite the growing consensus for change in how the opioid crisis is addressed, the Trump administration has mostly doubled down on old ideas about getting tough on crime. For example, Donald Trump sees border control as a crucial element in the crisis. In his 2019 budget plan, he cited the building of an $18 billion border wall with Mexico as an important way to stop the flow of heroin, fentanyl, and other illicit opioids into the United States. Trump has also stressed his belief in law enforcement as a solution. "My take is you have to get really, really tough, really mean with the drug pushers and the drug dealers,"[40] says Trump. At one point he endorsed the death penalty for drug dealers who sell opioids used in a fatal overdose.

In November 2017 a commission set up by the Trump administration issued a report with more than fifty recommendations on how to deal with the opioid crisis. Health experts agreed with many of the commission's findings. Among the more useful suggestions was creating block grants to help states get prompt federal funding for opioid abuse programs; requiring health care providers to take special classes on opioids before they can renew their federal licenses to prescribe; and setting up drug courts in all ninety-three judicial districts to help those arrested for possession get treatment instead of a prison sentence.

In October 2018 Congress passed a bill that, among other things, promised a crackdown on illicit mailings of fentanyl and support for new nonaddictive therapies for pain. While such laws are helpful, experts say they do not go far enough. "The data keeps showing us we have more and more people dying," says Chuck Ingoglia, senior vice president of public policy at the National Council for Behavioral Health, "so what's the reluctance to actually spend money and actually do something?"[41]

A Lifesaving Drug

One item that police and emergency workers are using in overdose cases has a value far beyond its cost—it frequently saves lives on the brink. Naloxone is a drug that can quickly reverse

The Angel Program

A town forum held in 2015 changed the way the Gloucester, Massachusetts, police force addressed the opioid crisis. Worried about the growing problem of overdose deaths, residents urged authorities to offer addicts compassion, not punishment. This fit with a changing consensus among experts that opioid addiction is more an issue of health than crime.

Police Chief Leonard Campanello set up the Angel program, an amnesty effort for addicts. Any opioid addict who walked into the Gloucester police station, surrendered drug paraphernalia, and asked for help was promised that no criminal charges would be levied. Instead, the person would receive immediate help aimed at entering a detox and recovery center. Assistance was provided by one of more than fifty so-called angels—local volunteers with experience in aid for addicts. Local businesses chipped in with discounted naloxone and free rides to treatment centers. Campanello noted that the Angel program cost about $55 per addict, compared to $220 to arrest and hold an addict in jail for one day. Soon police departments in several other states were starting their own versions of the program.

Today a nonprofit group helps support Angel programs in Gloucester and in two hundred sixty other police departments in thirty states. With more deadly opioids like fentanyl on the streets, the number of overdoses is still on the rise. Yet many recovering addicts credit the Angel program for their survival. "They're doing God's work over there," says Richard Naugle, an opioid addict in Gloucester. "How do you repay someone for saving your life?"

Quoted in Elise Amendola, "As Opioid Overdoses Rise, Pioneering Police Effort Evolves," CBS News, July 24, 2017. www.cbsnews.com.

---

the effects of an opioid overdose. Marketed under the name Narcan, among others, naloxone offers a second chance to opioid users who otherwise would almost certainly die from an opioid overdose.

A typical case unfolded in May 2018 in Enid, Oklahoma. Police sergeant John Robinson and two other officers were responding to a 911 call when they discovered a woman lying on the floor of her living room, in a stupor and barely breathing. Her husband, who had made the emergency call, confirmed she was on opioids. Following a quick check of her pulse and shallow breathing, Robinson administered a dose of the nasal spray Narcan just as he had been trained to do. He kept an eye on his watch as an ambulance crew arrived and began moving the woman into the vehicle. Robinson was taught to spray a second dose of the drug if the victim did not respond within three minutes. However, shortly after being lifted into the ambulance, the woman suddenly woke up, became alert, and began to breathe more normally.

This was the first time the Enid police or fire department had used one of the new rescue kits received from the Oklahoma Department of Mental Health Substance Abuse Services. Each kit contains two doses of naloxone. The officers' training proved decisive in the emergency call. "Certainly, with the quick thinking on [Robinson's] part, he saved this woman's life," says Lieutenant Eric Holtzclaw. "Minutes count when you're talking about brain injury."[42]

A Tool That Makes a Difference

Officers and medical workers across the nation are pleased to have an opioid blocker that is actually making a difference in the crisis. According to the federal agency Emergency Medical Services, naloxone has a 93 percent success rate in reviving victims of opioid overdose. Stories about naloxone's effectiveness are often in the news. For instance, in July 2018 singer Demi Lovato narrowly avoided a fatal overdose at her Hollywood home when emergency personnel arrived to administer Narcan. Experts on opioid abuse consider naloxone such an important safeguard they recommend that addicts, their spouses, or family members keep the drug on hand in case of an incident. Even opioid users who have kicked the habit are urged to have a rescue kit. In most states naloxone can be purchased over the counter without a prescription at pharmacies and national drugstore chains.

Naloxone dates back to 1971, when it was first approved by the FDA. The drug acts by binding to opioid receptors in the brain. This area of the brain is also in control of respiration, which

Singer Demi Lovato performs in Amsterdam in June 2018. One month later, she narrowly avoided a fatal opioid overdose when emergency personnel arrived to administer the opioid blocker Narcan.

is why a heavy dose of opioids can slow a user's breathing and even stop it altogether. When naloxone is administered after an overdose, it serves to block the effects of opioids. This allows normal breathing to be restored, reversing the overdose. According to Dr. Kelly Clark, president of the American Society of Addiction Medicine's board of directors, "As long as that naloxone is sitting in that receptor, other opioids can't get in there and activate it."[43] For years naloxone could only be delivered through a needle injection to a muscle in the victim's arm, thigh, or buttocks. The nasal spray version has made the drug much easier to administer. Naloxone is also safe to use when emergency personnel are not certain why a person is unresponsive. If the person has overdosed on a non-opioid drug or has passed out due to some other condition, administering naloxone will not revive him or her, but at the same time it does no harm.

In states where naloxone can be obtained without a prescription, police officials are using federal grant money to equip officers with Narcan kits and train them for proper use. Priced at forty dollars for a kit that is usable for only three or four months, Narcan is expensive for money-strapped departments that see lots of overdoses. Nonetheless, medical experts and law enforcement officials say the results justify the cost. Some police and emergency personnel have also voiced another reason for carrying the kits: personal safety. In the chaos of a drug scene,

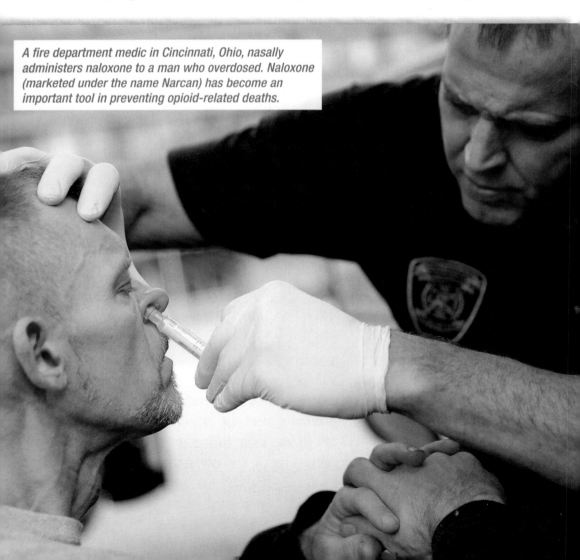

A fire department medic in Cincinnati, Ohio, nasally administers naloxone to a man who overdosed. Naloxone (marketed under the name Narcan) has become an important tool in preventing opioid-related deaths.

officers face the possibility of a random needle stick or inhalation of airborne opioid powder. Federal agents tell stories of drug busts in which suspects threw powdered opioids in the air so that agents would ingest them. When the opioids could be lethal fentanyl or carfentanil, authorities need naloxone available to protect themselves. Doug Wyllie, an expert on police training and public safety, says officers should take heed: "Naloxone . . . is as important to your safety and survival as your vest, your hands-on skills, or your sidearm."[44]

> "Naloxone . . . is as important to your safety and survival as your vest, your hands-on skills, or your sidearm."[44]
>
> —Doug Wyllie, an expert on police training and public safety

Community Policing

Police may have new tools and methods to deal with the opioid crisis, but traditional policing still has an important role to play. In fact, many officers today see themselves as part old-fashioned cop on the beat and part social worker. By establishing good relations with neighborhood residents, officers can take steps to get drug dealers off the streets and offer addicts the treatment they need.

Sometimes police can employ old-fashioned investigation plus networking to identify opioid dealers and put them out of business. Police in High Point, North Carolina, have used a community-based approach with success. First, they identified four neighborhoods most prone to drug sales and set up surveillance by undercover officers and informants. This brought to light key dealers in the drug trade. Those who had committed violent felonies were prosecuted, but nonviolent dealers were offered a bargain: If caught selling again, they would immediately be arrested, but if they agreed to enter a community-service program, they could receive housing, employment, a food and clothing allowance, and drug treatment. The approach has been adopted by police departments in several states.

The opioid epidemic has also placed new burdens on police because of all the related consequences they must deal with every day. Besides street sales and frequent overdose, there is violence between gangs, petty crimes by users to support their habit, and child abuse and neglect in drug-riddled families. Because of the dangers associated with the opioid trade, emergency responders often wait for police to arrive before entering a neighborhood thought to be unsafe. Officers can also help users through so-called harm-reduction programs. These include distributing Narcan to addicts and getting them into needle-exchange programs that help prevent hepatitis C and HIV. Police can also distribute

Narcan Versus Fentanyl

For police, the ultimate test for Narcan, the nasal spray version of naloxone, is to revive victims of fentanyl, among the most potent of synthetic opioids. The chances of overdosing on fentanyl are greater and the effects take place more quickly than with other opioids. Fentanyl sold on the streets may be an even more deadly nonpharmaceutical type—something cooked up to a vicious potency in an illicit lab. Moreover, the likelihood that fentanyl is mixed with heroin or other painkillers helps complicate the situation. Officers and emergency personnel know the dangers fentanyl presents to even longtime opioid abusers. The victim becomes confused or is gripped by seizures, with choking sounds, lips or nails turning blue, and pupils reduced to pinpoints. Slowed breathing and unresponsiveness quickly follow, with death only minutes away.

Narcan can reverse overdoses of fentanyl, but only if administered promptly. Because of fentanyl's potency, the CDC warns that multiple doses of naloxone may be required. If the user has taken an overdose of a non-opioid sedative such as Xanax laced with fentanyl, naloxone will address only the fentanyl's deadly effects. Once the overdose is reversed, the victim may remain confused and even combative for a while. The victim should receive immediate medical care, since the naloxone can wear off, causing the overdose condition to return. Yet the satisfaction for police and first responders lies in making a difference: seeing a limp, seemingly lifeless victim of fentanyl revive.

test strips so users can detect fentanyl in opioid mixtures. And like QRTs, neighborhood cops can sometimes direct addicts into inpatient or outpatient facilities for special care. "The people who overdose are citizens of the community, deserving of protection and service from the police," according to Arthur Rizer and Carrie Wade, policy experts for security and crime reduction. "Forsaking them will not reduce drug use. It will simply cost lives."[45]

Law enforcement experts stress that police cannot arrest their way out of the opioid crisis. Police departments in the hardest-hit areas are adopting new measures, such as rapid response teams, to deal with opioid addiction on a more personal level. Although traditional policing still has its place, these new approaches show great promise in rolling back the opioid epidemic in America.

> "The people who overdose are citizens of the community, deserving of protection and service from the police. Forsaking them will not reduce drug use. It will simply cost lives."[45]
>
> —Arthur Rizer and Carrie Wade, policy experts for security and crime reduction

CHAPTER FIVE

Treating the Opioid Problem

At age sixty-five, Joseph Purvis dreaded going on Medicare. The Gaithersburg, Maryland, resident has battled addiction to prescription painkillers and heroin for years and depends on methadone treatment to stabilize his addiction and help him function. The problem was that although Medicare provided coverage for opioid treatment, it did not pay for methadone. Only drugs that could be dispensed in a retail pharmacy fit Medicare's Part D prescription coverage. "I was terrified that I might have to leave the [methadone] program," says Purvis. "There's no way I wanted to go back to addiction on the streets."[46]

However, in October 2018 seniors like Purvis received some good news from an unlikely source: the US Congress. Under the SUPPORT for Patients and Communities Act, a bipartisan bill to address the opioid crisis, Medicare coverage was expanded to include methadone treatment. Health care experts, especially those who deal in issues that affect older Americans, hailed the change as a commonsense response to the crisis. But supporters such as Representative Elijah Cummings of Maryland also urged that much more needs to be done. "Unless we significantly expand funding and resources for treatment, this national crisis will continue to worsen," says Cummings. "This epidemic is killing 134 people a day, but only 1 in 10 people with the disease are getting treatment."[47]

Emphasis on Treatment and Recovery

Medical professionals who see opioid addicts daily emphasize that anger, blame, and scorn do little to solve the problem. What addicts need is an emphasis on treatment and recovery. Those affected range from very young to very old. Some seniors may have developed a tolerance to opioids over many years, which led them to take higher doses for pain relief and thereby fall into addiction. Others, like Purvis, may be looking for a way out after years of taking street drugs. Whatever the causes, in 2016 opioid overdoses killed more than thirteen hundred Americans age sixty-five or older. About three hundred thousand Medicare patients have been diagnosed as opioid addicts, with ninety thousand more considered at high risk. Previously, more than twenty-five thousand Medicare patients nationwide either had to pay eighty dollars a week out of pocket for methadone or depend on state-run programs for treatment. A simple step like Medicare expansion can not only improve lives but save them.

States that have revamped their treatment programs—including Hawaii, Massachusetts, Oklahoma, Vermont, and Wyoming—are already seeing falling rates of opioid addiction and overdose. Health officials in these states realize willpower alone is not enough for an opioid addict to change his or her life. They are finding ways to get addicts the medicines and professional help they need to get on the path to recovery.

> "I was terrified that I might have to leave the [methadone] program. There's no way I wanted to go back to addiction on the streets."[46]
>
> —Joseph Purvis, age sixty-five, recovering heroin addict

Medication-Assisted Treatment and Withdrawal

Health experts agree that one of the best ways to get users off opioids is medication-assisted treatment (MAT). This is the use of substitution drugs such as methadone, Suboxone, and naltrexone to wean addicts from painkillers, heroin, and synthetic opioids like fentanyl. This approach shows more promise than traditional twelve-step programs to treat addiction. Multiple studies indicate that MAT is safe and effective. Yet public health officials warn that funding for this program continues to lag far behind what is needed in opioid-plagued areas.

A Georgia woman takes a dose of methadone in an effort to wean herself off opioids. Methadone is one of the substances used in medication-assisted treatment, which is considered a safe and effective method of ending addiction.

The idea behind MAT is to help opioid addicts avoid the agonies of withdrawal as they try to get clean. Withdrawal symptoms are the result of changes in the addict's brain and body due to heavy use of opioids. A user's brain develops a tolerance for opioids, meaning that higher and more frequent doses are needed to get the same euphoric effect. Finally, the drug is needed simply to stave off withdrawal.

When a person fails to take the usual dose of oxycodone or heroin, he or she experiences a powerful craving for the drug, both psychological and physical. Focus on obtaining another fix becomes all consuming. The body undergoes symptoms that resemble flu-like illness. They include insomnia, anxiety, dilated pupils, muscle aches, fever, sweating, nausea, vomiting, and diarrhea. Should the vomiting and diarrhea persist without treatment, the person may become dangerously dehydrated and even subject to heart failure. "I don't know how to describe withdrawal. It's like the worst flu you've ever had in your life—and then multiply that by 1,000," says Todd, a longtime heroin addict. "There's a scraping inside your brain. You're willing to do anything to feel better."[48]

The Use of Antiaddiction Drugs

Recovering heroin addicts like Joseph Purvis rely on methadone to avoid withdrawal and get through the day. The pink-colored liquid is a long-acting synthetic opioid, meaning it does not have the instant narcotic kick of heroin. Created in the 1940s as a battlefield narcotic, methadone stops pain and slows breathing. It has a sedative effect, which makes it a helpful detox drug to counter the anxiety and depression that accompany withdrawal from heroin. Since methadone reduces bowel activity, it can also work against the severe diarrhea that is common with heroin withdrawal. To begin treatment, doctors administer precise 10- to 20-milligram doses of methadone and increase dosage steadily by 10 milligrams until the withdrawal symptoms are controlled.

> "I don't know how to describe withdrawal. It's like the worst flu you've ever had in your life—and then multiply that by 1,000. . . . You're willing to do anything to feel better."[48]
>
> —Todd, a longtime heroin addict

Then, in theory, the methadone doses are reduced until the patient is drug free. In reality, methadone, which itself is addictive, often becomes part of a continuing, long-term maintenance program for hard-core addicts. Regardless, studies show other positive effects from making methadone treatment available. For hard-hit communities, it can decrease both heroin usage and the spread of infectious diseases such as HIV and hepatitis C by shared needles.

Suboxone is a synthetic opioid created expressly to combat opioid addiction. Eighty percent of the drug is buprenorphine, a mild synthetic opioid, and 20 percent is naloxone, the anti-overdose medication that blocks opioid receptors in the brain. Buprenorphine does not activate receptors to the same degree as methadone, making it much less addictive. It is long acting like methadone, maintaining its effect in the body for up to sixty hours. However, its most potent effect tops out with a moderate dose, so that addicts are not tempted to increase the dosage. Thus, Suboxone, a tablet approved by the FDA in 2002, has become a popular drug for clinics that provide medication-assisted opioid treatment. In general, its milder profile works best with patients who do not have a long history with opioids and have not developed a high tolerance for them. Nonetheless, some hardcore addicts find it beneficial as well.

Suboxone has become a vital maintenance drug for those suffering from addiction. According to research, use of Suboxone results in 45 percent fewer emergency room visits for recovering opioid

A Tennessee pain specialist works with a patient who has chronic back pain. The specialist is one of relatively few doctors who can prescribe Suboxone, a synthetic opioid that is less addictive than other pain meds and more effective in relieving pain.

addicts. Amanda S., a recovering heroin addict who lives in Michigan, swears by Suboxone. After kicking a three-year heroin habit, she became hooked on the prescription painkiller Opana while taking it for fibromyalgia, a painful nerve disease. She suffered severe withdrawal symptoms from the pain pills and checked into a mental hospital. When doctors gave her Suboxone, Amanda felt like a new person. "I felt like I could finally get out of bed, function and take a shower!" she says. "I was impressed that my head wasn't foggy and I didn't feel 'high.' That feeling hasn't changed over time, and because it helps with my fibromyalgia so much, I take less medicine now, than I ever did."[49] She has continued to use Suboxone for the past eight years.

> "I felt like I could finally get out of bed, function and take a shower! I was impressed that my head wasn't foggy and I didn't feel 'high.' That feeling hasn't changed over time, and because it helps with my fibromyalgia so much, I take less medicine now, than I ever did."[49]
>
> —Amanda S., on the antiaddiction drug Suboxone

Need for Licensing and Training

With so many experts and recovering addicts praising Suboxone, there have been calls for it to be more widely prescribed. Studies show the drug offers opioid addicts more hope for recovery than nonmedication treatments such as twelve-step programs. Yet communities hit hardest by the opioid epidemic say too few local doctors are able—or willing—to prescribe buprenorphine, the main ingredient in Suboxone.

Although more than nine hundred thousand doctors in the United States are authorized to prescribe opioid painkillers, only a fraction have the proper waiver to offer patients Suboxone. A waiver is obtained by completing eight hours of training on how to prescribe and dispense buprenorphine, the main ingredient in Suboxone. The need for qualified prescribers is felt most in small towns and rural areas where opioid addiction is growing. And despite positive reports, many doctors are reluctant to get a waiver or to use it once they have it. They fear prescribing addicted patients another opioid amid a possible backlash. Many refuse to devote sufficient time to studying the drug and feel they lack expertise in its dosage and side effects. Screening patients and getting them started on Suboxone also takes a great deal of time. Doctors need specially trained assistants to help with the process. Nonetheless, prescribing Suboxone can smooth the treatment routine for doctors and patients alike. Kelly Eagen, a primary care physician in a run-down section of San Francisco, enlists the help of a local clinic to screen her addicted patients to see if Suboxone treatment is appropriate for them. "When the patient is handed back to me, I know that the person is not at risk for imminent relapse," says Eagen. "They're the easiest patients I have."[50]

Congress's recent opioid bill promises to increase patient access to Suboxone. The bill expands the ability of nurse practitioners and physician's assistants with waivers to prescribe the drug. It also allows other health care workers who obtain waivers, such as certified nurse specialists and certified nurse midwives, to offer prescriptions for five years. Health experts applaud the move as a lifesaver for recovering addicts.

Use of Suboxone and other antiaddiction drugs must also overcome another prejudice. Some physicians have moral qualms about offering opioids to addicts as a form of treatment. They say this approach only substitutes one addictive drug for another. In their view opioid addicts should first be counseled to go "cold turkey" and stop all use of painkillers. MAT should only be used as a last resort.

Expanding Funding for Treatment

Health officials stress that more funding is needed to treat opioid addicts. An important source of funds is Medicaid, the joint federal and state program that pays medical costs for low-income individuals and families. The Affordable Care Act sought to expand Medicaid across the country to improve health care options for

The Importance of Getting Treatment

For opioid addicts without means, merely getting accepted into a treatment center can be a challenge. Steve, a recovering heroin addict from New Jersey, lacked insurance or cash when he sought placement at a rehab facility. The first step, he says, was to call and leave a message. It was the first of several repeat calls. In order to pass the first test, he had to show the staff he was serious about getting clean. Eventually, he got lucky and received a return call. A person at the center made him an offer of help, but only if he could get there within four or five hours. He was able to make the deadline. However, someone who is already high with no car or helpful friend might well miss out entirely.

Those who miss out on treatment typically go back on the streets. Many of them overdose again and again, until finally there is no opioid blocker available in time. Steve often thinks about the waste of potentially productive citizens who have become unemployable. They fall into opioid addiction and wind up in jail or dead in an alleyway. "Consider the extra burden on Medicaid, welfare programs, and homeless shelters," he says. "More important, forget all of those expenses and simply consider what it means for millions of families to have loved ones in the grip of untreated addiction." As Steve knows all too well, the future for an opioid addict depends on finding one's way into a treatment center.

Quoted in Lela Moore, "Clean, Sober and $41,000 Deep in Out-of-Pocket Addiction Recovery Costs," *New York Times*, July 26, 2018. www.nytimes.com.

the impoverished, but some states rejected the plan. In states that accepted expansion, Medicaid funds support community health centers and nonprofit clinics that represent the front lines in the fight against opioid addiction. Almost half of these health centers provide antiaddiction drugs as part of their MAT programs. For those that offer drugs, nearly 90 percent provide buprenorphine. Medicaid expansion states are also more likely to offer naltrexone, a longer-acting MAT drug that requires fewer visits from addicted patients.

In addition, Medicaid funding pays for counseling and psychological treatment. According to the American Academy of

Addiction Psychiatry, 50 to 70 percent of substance-abuse patients also have issues with depression, posttraumatic stress, or other mental health problems. One of the most effective solutions is for recovering addicts to live in institutions for mental disease, where they can receive psychological help along with MAT. Here again the recent opioid bill made an important change. The bill abolished a decades-old rule that banned Medicaid funding for drug patients in mental hospitals with more than sixteen beds. "In the Medicaid field, with reimbursement not robust, no one could make it really well without cobbling together grants and other funding," says Shawn Ryan, chief medical officer of the outpatient treatment center BrightView in Cincinnati, Ohio. "The removal of [the ban] could really help."[51]

Expansion of Medicaid funding has many advocates among health experts, but some note another issue it raises. Although Medicaid money is essential for treatment of opioid addiction, it is also used to purchase prescription painkillers for low-income users. Critics say Medicaid continues to feed the very problem it is trying to solve.

Prevention and Pain Management

Concern about the opioid crisis is prompting new approaches to prevention and pain management. Some initiatives are quite radical. For example, the Oregon Health Authority has prepared a plan that takes aim at the overprescribing of opioids. Starting in 2020 physicians would be required to gradually cut off doses of OxyContin, Percocet, and Vicodin. The state's Medicaid program would also end opioid coverage for patients with chronic pain. Coverage would instead be extended to alternative treatments such as acupuncture, yoga, and physical therapy.

Since it was announced, the Oregon plan has drawn sharp criticism from health experts and patients alike. Steve Hix, an Albany, Oregon, resident who is mostly bedridden with spine injuries, fought through the pain to protest at a public meeting on the plan. "I'm very sad for the people who OD'd," says Hix.

"But what's that got to do with me?"[52] In a national newspaper column, medical scholars Sally Satel and Stefan Kertesz admit the prescribing problem is real but express dismay at such a brutal dismissal of pain relief. "There is no question that some patients have abused Medicaid to purchase fistfuls of opioids through illegal pill mills or to scam physicians into writing prescriptions for medication they resell," they write. "Medicaid needs to protect against such fraud, but Oregon officials should not swing a scythe where a scalpel will suffice."[53]

> "I'm very sad for the people who OD'd. But what's that got to do with me?"[52]
>
> —Steve Hix, a patient who takes opioids to deal with pain from spine injuries

People who suffer chronic pain are often urged to try yoga, physical therapy, and other alternatives to opioid painkillers. In some cases, however, legitimate use of pain meds is being curtailed because of concerns about addiction.

Texting Support for Opioid Abusers

A new tool to support recovering opioid addicts is as simple as a concerned text message. Researchers at Washington University School of Medicine and Epharmix, a St. Louis–based digital health company, have developed a new automated text service to help opioid addicts avoid relapse and maintain therapy treatments. The service sends automatic text messages and phone calls asking patients how they are feeling or if they are verging on relapse. A panic button is provided so patients can send for immediate assistance. Not only does the service help health care workers monitor each recovering addict, it can also lower medical costs by reducing the need for in-person checkups. A recovery clinic can keep track of more patients in less time overall.

Avik Som, chief medical officer at Epharmix, got the idea for the text service from similar technologies used to manage chronic diseases such as diabetes and hypertension. The service aims to supplement cognitive behavioral therapy and other forms of treatment used to fight opioid addiction. "This is not meant to replace important programs or face-to-face contact between patients and providers," says Som. "Rather, it is an additional tool that is affordable and immediate. . . . Patients reported feeling more connected to health-care providers." So far the new service has been tested only on a small scale. However, early results are encouraging, with half of the twenty-one patients reporting no opioid use after three months.

Quoted in Kristina Sauerwein, "Text Messaging Tool May Help Fight Opioid Epidemic," Washington University School of Medicine in St. Louis, April 17, 2018. https://medicine.wustl.edu.

Satel and Kertesz highlight what some experts see as another danger related to the opioid crisis. In the effort to curtail the prescribing of painkillers, health officials may neglect the legitimate pain-relief needs of ordinary patients. As Satel and Kertesz point out, risk of opioid abuse and overdose is actually low among users who do not suffer from mental illness or do not mix opioids with alcohol and other drugs. It would be ironic indeed if doctors' original concern to provide pain relief—with OxyContin and other opioids—should ultimately lead to a fear of prescribing painkillers due to the risk of addiction.

Health experts stress the importance of treatment and recovery in confronting the opioid crisis. Instead of blame and punishment, addicts benefit most from therapies like MAT. Federal and state funds make up a vital lifeline for treatment centers, but more help is needed. Without a concerted effort to rescue opioid addicts and prevent more addiction, communities and families will continue to be plagued by this crisis.

Introduction: A Heavy Toll on Families and Communities

1. Quoted in Bob Hille, "Rice DE Blain Padgett's Death Caused by Synthetic Opioid," *Sporting News*, June 20, 2018. www.sportingnews.com.
2. Quoted in Cristina Corbin, "Family's Fentanyl Tragedy Underscores 'Mind-Boggling' Opioid Crisis in New Hampshire," Fox News, June 17, 2018. www.foxnews.com.
3. Quoted in Corbin, "Family's Fentanyl Tragedy Underscores 'Mind-Boggling' Opioid Crisis in New Hampshire."
4. Quoted in Robin Young, "Here's What West Virginia Is Doing to Address the Opioid Crisis," *Here & Now*, WBUR, May 11, 2018. www.wbur.org.

Chapter One: The Roots of the Opioid Crisis

5. Quoted in Colin Dwyer, "Massachusetts Sues OxyContin Maker Purdue Pharma, Saying It 'Peddled Falsehoods,'" NPR, June 13, 2018. www.npr.org.
6. Quoted in Jamie Satterfield, "OxyContin Maker: Doctors, Patients, Drug Dealers to Blame for Opioid Epidemic," *Knoxville (TN) News Sentinel*, August 18, 2018. www.knoxnews.com.
7. Quoted in Harriet Ryan et al., "'You Want a Description of Hell?' OxyContin's 12-Hour Problem," *Los Angeles Times*, May 5, 2016. www.latimes.com.
8. Quoted in Patrick Radden Keefe, "The Family That Built an Empire of Pain," *New Yorker*, October 30, 2017. www.newyorker.com.
9. Quoted in Ryan et al., "'You Want a Description of Hell?'"
10. Quoted in Beth Macy, "'They Were All Lawyered Up and Rudy Giuliani'd Up,'" Politico, August 5, 2018. www.politico.com.
11. Quoted in Macy, "'They Were All Lawyered Up and Rudy Giuliani'd Up.'"

12. Quoted in Macy, "'They Were All Lawyered Up and Rudy Giuliani'd Up.'"
13. Quoted in Brett Kelman, "These Nashville Doctors Were Running Pill Mills. Purdue Pharma Sold to Them Anyway," *Nashville Tennessean*, July 11, 2018. www.tennessean.com.

Chapter Two: From Pain Pills to Heroin and Fentanyl

14. Quoted in David Browne, "Music's Fentanyl Crisis: Inside the Drug That Killed Prince and Tom Petty," *Rolling Stone*, June 20, 2018. www.rollingstone.com.
15. Quoted in Browne, "Music's Fentanyl Crisis."
16. Quoted in Daniella Silva, "Prince Died After Taking Fake Vicodin Laced with Fentanyl, Prosecutor Says," NBC News, April 19, 2018. www.nbcnews.com.
17. Quoted in Browne, "Music's Fentanyl Crisis."
18. German Lopez, "The Maker of OxyContin Tried to Make It Harder to Misuse. It May Have Led to More Heroin Deaths," Vox, April 16, 2018. www.vox.org.
19. Roger Chriss, "OxyContin, Heroin, and the Opioid Crisis," Pain News Network, July 3, 2018. www.painnewsnetwork.org.
20. Quoted in Jessica Bruder, "The Worst Drug Crisis in American History," *New York Times*, July 31, 2018. www.nytimes.com.
21. Quoted in Harrison Jacobs, "Prescriptions for Painkillers Brought About the Explosion in Heroin Use in America's Suburbs," Business Insider, March 11, 2017. www.businessinsider.com.
22. Quoted in Jacobs, "Prescriptions for Painkillers Brought About the Explosion in Heroin Use in America's Suburbs."
23. Quoted in Michael O'Brien, "Fentanyl Changed the Opioid Epidemic. Now It's Getting Worse," *Rolling Stone*, August 31, 2018. www.rollingstone.com.
24. Quoted in Nicole Lewis et al., "Fentanyl Linked to Thousands of Urban Overdose Deaths," *Washington Post*, August 15, 2017. www.washingtonpost.com.

25. Quoted in Rick McCrabb, "Ohio Mother Who Died of Drug Overdose Was 'Thrown Away like a Bag of Trash,' Family Says," *Middletown (OH) Journal-News*, August 7, 2018. www.journal-news.com.

26. Quoted in Ed Richter, "The Middletown Community Talked Honestly Last Night About the Human Costs of the Opioid Epidemic," *Middletown (OH) Journal-News*, February 13, 2018. www.journal-news.com.

27. Quoted in Jeanna Smialek and Patricia Laya, "The New Face of American Unemployment," Bloomberg, February 7, 2017. www.bloomberg.com.

28. Quoted in Paige Winfield Cunningham, "The Health 202: Appalachian Death from Drug Overdoses Far Outpace Nation's," *Washington Post*, October 30, 2017. www.washingtonpost.com.

29. Quoted in Kyle Younker and Taylor Harrison, "Appalachia's Coal Comeback Collides with Grim Opioid Reality," Debtwire, January 12, 2018. http://investigations.debtwire.com.

30. Quoted in Harrison Jacobs, "Here's Why the Opioid Epidemic Is So Bad in West Virginia—the State with the Highest Overdose Rate in the US," Business Insider, May 1, 2016. www.businessinsider.com.

31. Quoted in Veronica Volk, "Opioid Addiction Can Set Off Chain Reaction Through Family," WSKG, April 12, 2018. https://wskg.org.

32. Quoted in Volk, "Opioid Addiction Can Set Off Chain Reaction Through Family."

33. Quoted in Sarah Jane Tribble, "For Babies of the Opioid Crisis, Best Care May Be Mom's Recovery," NPR, May 8, 2018. www.npr.org.

34. Quoted in Tribble, "For Babies of the Opioid Crisis, Best Care May Be Mom's Recovery."

35. Quoted in Yuki Noguchi, "Anguished Families Shoulder the Biggest Burdens of Opioid Addiction," NPR, April 18, 2018. www.npr.org.

Chapter Four: Policing the Opioid Crisis

36. Quoted in Kara Leigh Lofton, "Quick Response Teams Aim to Get More Opioid Overdose Patients into Treatment," West Virginia Public Broadcasting, April 3, 2018. www.wvpublic.org.

37. Quoted in Lofton, "Quick Response Teams Aim to Get More Opioid Overdose Patients into Treatment."

38. Quoted in ADM Board, "How Does a Quick Response Team Make a Difference?," March 20, 2017. www.admboard.org.

39. Nan Whaley, "Opioid Epidemic Requires a New Perspective on Addiction Treatment and New Solutions," *USA Today*, June 22, 2018. www.usatoday.com.

40. Quoted in German Lopez, "30 Experts Were Asked How They'd Fight the Opioid Crisis. None Mentioned a Border Wall," Vox, February 14, 2018. www.vox.com.

41. Quoted in Brianna Ehley, "Congress' Latest Opioid Bill Won't Solve the Crisis," Politico, September 17, 2018. www.politico.com.

42. Quoted in Cass Rains, "EPD Sergeant's Use of Narcan Saves Woman's Life," *Enid (OK) News & Eagle*, May 16, 2018. www.enidnews.com.

43. Quoted in Annamarya Scaccia, "Naloxone: How Overdose-Reversing Drug Saved Demi Lovato, Thousands More," *Rolling Stone*, August 7, 2018. www.rollingstone.com.

44. Doug Wyllie, "Why Every Cop Should Carry Naloxone," PoliceOne, June 19, 2017. www.policeone.com.

45. Arthur Rizer and Carrie Wade, "The Opioid Epidemic Is Changing Law Enforcement," *Newsday*, September 28, 2017. www.newsday.com.

Chapter Five: Treating the Opioid Problem

46. Quoted in Carla K. Johnson, "Opioid Treatment Gap in Medicare: Methadone Clinics," *U.S. News & World Report*, April 24, 2018. www.usnews.com.

47. Quoted in Abby Vesoulis, "Opioid Bill Shows Congress Can Still Work Together," *Time*, October 6, 2018. www.time.com.

48. Quoted in Jessica Ravitz, "Inside the Secret Lives of Functioning Heroin Addicts," CNN, February 27, 2018. www.cnn .com.
49. Quoted in Kali Lux, "From Heroin User to Health Advocate: Suboxone Success Story Amanda S.," Workit Health, January 30, 2018. www.workithealth.com.
50. Quoted in Christine Vestal, "Deadly Bias," Pew Trusts, January 15, 2016. www.pewtrusts.org.
51. Quoted in Susannah Luthi, "Medicaid Payment for Opioid Treatment Embroiled in Politics Over Loosening Restrictions," *Modern Healthcare*, May 16, 2018. www.modernhealthcare .com.
52. Quoted in KVAL, "Oregon May Limit Opioid Prescriptions to Combat Overprescribing—and Addiction," July 26, 2018. www.kval.com.
53. Sally Satel and Stefan Kertesz, "Oregon Overshoots on Opioids," *Wall Street Journal*, August 17, 2018. www.wsj.com.

American Association of Colleges of Nursing
655 K St. NW, Suite 750
Washington, DC 20001
website: www.aacnnursing.org

The American Association of Colleges of Nursing is a nonpartisan group that serves to educate and advocate for nursing education, research, and practice. Its website features fact sheets on the opioid epidemic and so-called Opioids Tool Kits to keep nurses and health care workers up-to-date on opioids and managing chronic pain.

American Medical Association (AMA)
AMA Plaza
330 N. Wabash Ave., Suite 39300
Chicago, IL 60611
website: www.ama-assn.org

The AMA promotes meaningful innovation to create a better health care system for patients and physicians. It recently released a report on how physicians in the United States are leading the effort to reverse the opioid epidemic. The AMA website also includes reports from its Opioid Task Force on patient stories and programs to monitor prescription painkillers.

Brookings Institution
1775 Massachusetts Ave. NW
Washington, DC 20036
website: www.brookings.edu

The Brookings Institution is a progressive think tank based in Washington, DC. It studies and makes policy recommendations on many issues, including the opioid crisis. The Brookings website features in-depth articles such as "A What-Works Approach to the Opioid Crisis" and "The Far-Reaching Effects of the US Opioid Crisis."

Center for American Progress (CAP)

1333 H St. NW
Washington, DC 20005
website: www.americanprogress.org

CAP is an independent policy institute that supports expansion of federal health coverage to treat opioid addiction and prevent opioid abuse. The CAP website contains articles on how the opioid crisis affects minorities and how federal budget cuts could harm those who need treatment for opioid addiction.

DrugAbuse.com

Recovery Brands, LLC
517 Fourth Ave., Suite 401
San Diego, CA 92101
website: https://drugabuse.com

DrugAbuse.com provides information and resources to people struggling with addiction. Featured on this site are details about trends in treatment of opioid addiction, as well as developments in national and state drug policies. It also provides information about drug abuse programs in all fifty states, and advice on how to get treatment for opioid abuse.

National Institute on Drug Abuse (NIDA)

Office of Science Policy and Communications
Public Information and Liaison Branch
6001 Executive Blvd., Room 5213, MSC 9561
Bethesda, MA 20892
website: www.drugabuse.gov

The NIDA's mission is to advance scientific knowledge on the causes and consequences of drug use and addiction. It works to apply science to improve individual and public health. The NIDA's website features extensive information on the opioid crisis, including the latest research and statistics on opioid abuse.

WebMD

website: www.webmd.com

WebMD provides valuable health information, tools for managing health, and in-depth medical news and features. Its website is a great source of information about the opioid epidemic, with features on painkilling drugs, heroin, fentanyl, buprenorphine, and other topics.

Books

Adam Bisaga and Karen Chernyaev, *Overcoming Opioid Addiction: The Authoritative Medical Guide for Patients, Families, Doctors, and Therapists*. New York: Experiment LLC, 2018.

Ryan Hampton, *Inside the Opioid Addiction Crisis—and How to End It*. New York: St. Martin's, 2018.

Beth Macy, *Dopesick: Dealers, Doctors, and the Drug Company That Addicted America*. New York: Little, Brown, 2018.

Hal Marcovitz, *The Opioid Epidemic*. San Diego, CA: ReferencePoint, 2018.

Tracey Helton Mitchell, *The Big Fix: Hope After Heroin*. Berkeley, CA: Seal, 2017.

Sam Quinones, *Dreamland: The True Tale of America's Opiate Epidemic*. New York: Bloomsbury, 2016.

Internet Sources

Jennifer Egan, "Children of the Opioid Epidemic," *New York Times Magazine*, May 9, 2018. www.nytimes.com.

William N. Evans and Ethan Lieber, "How the Reformulation of OxyContin Ignited the Heroin Epidemic," Cato Institute, August 15, 2018. www.cato.org.

Northpoint Washington, "What the Future Holds for Opioid Addiction Treatment in 2018 and Beyond," 2018. www.northpoint washington.com.

Margaret Talbot, "The Addicts Next Door," *New Yorker*, June 5 and 12, 2017. www.newyorker.com.

U.S. Department of Health and Human Services, "National Opioids Crisis: Help, Resources and Information." www.hhs.gov.

INDEX

Cover: Kamira/Shutterstock.com

 6: Leslie Plaza Johnson/Icon Sportswire DBA/Newscom
10: PureRadiancePhoto/Shutterstock.com
14: Associated Press
18: Associated Press
23: Maury Aaseng
27: C_KAWI/Shutterstock.com
28: Joshua Lott/Reuters/Newscom
34: Associated Press
37: Associated Press
40: Robert Cohen/TNS/Newscom
44: Associated Press
49: Ben Houdijk/Shutterstock.com
50: Associated Press
56: Associated Press
58: Associated Press
63: Joan Photo/Shutterstock.com